MAJOR

SHAITAN SINGH, PVC

THE MAN IN HALF LIGHT

A COMPLETE BIOGRAPHY BY

JAI SAMOTA

No part of this publication can be reproduced, stored in a retrieval system or transmitted in any form or by any means, electronic, mechanical, photocopying, recording or otherwise, without prior permission of the author. Rights of this book are reserved with the author.

Published by
PRABHAT PRAKASHAN PVT. LTD.
4/19 Asaf Ali Road,
New Delhi-110 002 (INDIA)
e-mail: prabhatbooks@gmail.com

ISBN 978-93-5562-609-7
MAJOR SHAITAN SINGH, PVC: THE MAN IN HALF LIGHT
A Complete Biography by Jai Samota

© Reserved

Edition
2025

Price
₹ 500 (Rupees Five Hundred Only)

Printed at
R-Tech Offset Printers, Delhi

"When I was researching about Major Shaitan Singh, PVC, I never thought it would be so hard to find out about 1962. I started finding people related to the war. While I talked to people, I sensed hesitation talking about the war. Some of them didn't even want to talk about the horrors of the war. Those dark nights with glowing flashes still haunt people. Those snow-clad white shining heights which we as tourists see and look so beautiful are nightmares for some of the bravest souls. Only they know what they've lost there, those white shining heights are actually red, red due to the blood of those who never came back. It is a story of pain which no one can understand."

Foreword

I had the unique privilege of serving with the late Maj Shaitan Singh, for two years at the Kumaon Regimental Centre, in the late 1950s and for about one and a half years in 13 Kumaon, before he met his heroic death in the Battle of Rezang La on November 18, 1962. The fact that I was commanding a company post at Magar Hill at one end of the Kailash Range while Rezang La was at the other end lends poignancy to my association and friendship with Maj Shaitan Singh. It is said that generally introverted soldiers do well in war. However I have not heard of anyone so utterly simple and gentle in normal life to have fought so bravely in action. This biography amply projects that apart from bravery, Maj Shaitan Singh displayed devotion to duty, while fighting against heavy odds. He also showed concern for the men in his command when he ordered the party evacuating him for medical attention, to leave him and save their own lives. A more deserving case for the award of Param Vir Chakra cannot be imagined.

I offer warm compliments to Mr Jai Samota for writing this biography. Barely in his twenties. Jai shows unusual maturity in dealing with his subject. He took infinite pains to dig out shreds of information about Maj Shaitan by approaching anyone and everyone even remotely connected with him. Thus the biography describes numerous incidents which together reflect Maj Shaitan's true character. I am sure this biography will be read avidly by the young generation who will draw inspiration to serve their country and motherland with patriotic zeal.

I wish all success to Jai Samota in future as a historian and biographer.

Brig Raghunath V Jatar (Retd)
Pune
August 26, 2023

❑

Author's Note

It was winter, I was travelling on a bus in Rajasthan – the "Land of Braves". While travelling, I came across a story of an Indian Army soldier, a warrior. The man was an Army company commander who belonged to Rajasthan. He fought an extraordinary battle 56 years ago from the day of my travel. His name was a slightly odd, which struck me because it was antithetical to his personality. I started reading more about him and came to know about his act of bravery on the battlefield.

Intrigued by his story, I began looking for his family. It was very difficult for me to contact his son.

You may find it amusing, but I finally got his contact via Google Maps. It took me more than six months to get in touch with his only son and another four months to visit him. It was my first time visiting a fallen soldier's family. For you to know, I was somewhat nervous, so I took Vikram Mehta, a dear friend, with me.

Mr Narpat Singh, the fallen soldier's son, greeted us with warmth. And here I was – before my hero's son.

Most of you would have heard or read about the legendary Battle of Rezang La but only a few people know about the life of the Hero of Rezang La beyond the battle. There are many articles, poems and songs written about him but there is no book written about him. I never thought of writing a book but while talking to Mr. Narpat Singh, I found the story so interesting that I decided to write a biography on his great father Maj Shaitan Singh, PVC. It was a momentous decision and probably the fastest and one of the best decisions of my life.

I had only one thing in mind, which was to only state facts no matter what happens. I contacted people from his family, his friends, and colleagues as well. Most of the people I spoke to are very old. Yet they remember their dear friend/colleague Shaitan Singh. At such an old age, many memories fade, but such was the aura of Shaitan Singh that people didn't forget anything about him.

I wanted readers to know about the life of this courageous man; and personally, I was curious as to what made such a calm person fight such a terrific battle.

I hope I can give my readers a perceptive insight of Major Shaitan Singh's life covering all the important events and happenings.

❑

Acknowledgements

I am forever indebted to Major Shaitan Singh for everything. Only due to him, I've come up with such a fascinating story. To Charlie Company I pay my sincere tributes.

I would like to thank my mother Manjula Samota for constantly supporting me and always praying for me during ups and downs and to my father Anil Kumar Samota for always supporting me and sending me to Rezang La and making sure I live my dream. I would like to thank my sister Anushree Samota who always made me believe in myself and kept saying that I would complete all my dreams one day. I also thank my sister Preeti Sahni and my cousins Mridul, Kanishk and Abhay Samota for advising me throughout the journey.

I am indebted to Mr. Narpat Singh son of Major Shaitan Singh, PVC who believed in me and supported me during the journey by providing all the information related to his beloved father. I am also thankful to Commandant Prithvi Singh (retd), younger brother of Major Shaitan Singh, PVC for sharing important information about their father, Lt Col Hem Singh, OBI and also for sharing some unheard stories about his loving brother. I would like to show my gratitude to Mr. Manvendra Singh Bhati, grand nephew of Major Shaitan Singh, PVC who helped me a lot in various ways during this journey by sharing stories and valuable information about his grand uncle and also I would like to thank him for taking me to Colonel Shivji Singh the only alive school and college senior of Major Shaitan Singh.

I'm thankful to Mr. Mahendra Singh Rathore, son of Mr. Mool Singh Rathore who welcomed me with so much affection and showed me Major Shaitan Singh's watch and also allowed me to read some letters written by his beloved Mamosa (maternal uncle).

I admire the efforts of Major Shaitan Singh's family to allow me to research the life of Major Shaitan Singh and provided me with every possible information, letters and photographs.

I convey my regards to the Kumaon Regiment and its Battalions specially Jangi and Rezang-La, one unit which forged him and another in which he proved his mettle. I'm grateful to IX Grenadiers, Mewar for their endless motivation.

I'm extremely thankful to my friend, Vikram Mehta who came with me to Jodhpur twice just because of my passion for Major Shaitan Singh, PVC and helped me during research.

I'm grateful to Colonel Shivji Singh (retd), the one hundred-years-old veteran and a school, college and unit senior of Major Shaitan Singh, PVC, for his valuable inputs for my research. Even at this age he remembers his company officer's personality as an affectionate person who was loved and respected by his troops.

I convey my deepest gratitude to Brigadier Raghunath V. Jatar (retd), the 90-years-old die hard Kumaoni veteran and the Delta Company Commander for always helping me during the research, one who helped me to contact various veterans and families and made this research easy for me. I also like to thank him for letting me stay with him during my visit to Rezang-La, Chushul.

I'm thankful to Major Bakhtawar Singh Brar and his son Major Manjeet Singh Brar (retd), Brigadier Prem Kumar (retd) and his wife Mrs Shobha who shared their experiences and stories related to Major Shaitan Singh, PVC with me. I would like to thank Brigadier S.P. Joshi (retd) of Regiment of the Artillery, Colonel S.P. Dua (retd) and Lt Col Prem Singh (retd) of Jat regiment for sharing some important anecdotes related to the 1962 war period.

I am deeply touched by the efforts made by the octogenarian veterans Honorary Captain Man Singh, Honorary Captain Chamu Singh Mehra, Honorary Captain Ram Chander Yadav, Havildar Nihal Singh, S.M., Havildar Asha Ram and Havildar Sahi Ram for providing me information about their commander Major Shaitan Singh, PVC and the battle of Rezang La.

I'm thankful to Mrs Sheela Lamba, wife of the late Brigadier B.S. Lamba and Mrs Rani Khanna, wife of the late Maj Gen R.K. Khanna for sharing their stories and anecdotes related to their husbands' colleague Major Shaitan Singh. I'm also thankful to Mrs. Pradanya Wakhle, wife of the late Major P.M. Wakhle for sharing some stories which she heard from her husband and for the unique photograph of Major Shaitan Singh during the Goa Liberation Operation.

I'm grateful to Lt Col N.S. Pathania (retd) and Mr Kamaljeet Singh Pathania both sons of Lt Col Kaman Singh, MVC for providing me with information about their father and 6 Kumaon.

Mrs Sunita Mukherjee and Major Har Amrit Singh Dhingra (retd), children of Colonel Hari Singh Dhingra, AVSM specially helped me by providing their valuable inputs, stories and photographs related to Major Shaitan Singh, PVC. I'm thankful to Lt Gen Ramesh Halgali son of Major G. Halgali for providing group photographs of Officers of 13 Kumaon and Major Shaitan Singh, PVC and for constantly motivating me. I would also like to convey my thanks to Mrs Promila Soam daughter of Lt Col Mukut Singh for telling me some stories about Major Shaitan Singh.

I convey my wishes to the Rezang La Shaurya Samiti for its dedication towards the families of Rezang La warriors. I especially like to thank Advocate Naresh Chouhan, Dr. R.C. Sharma and Honorary Captain Bhola Ram (retd) for hosting me at Rewari and helping me meet the veterans of Rezang La. I would like to thank Colonel NN Bhatia (retd) for initially helping me understand the battle of Rezang La.

I thank Mr Sajjan Singh, son of late AVM Chandan Singh, MVC, AVSM, VrC and his cousin Major General Kishan Singh (retd), son of the late Brigadier Hari Singh, AVSM for sharing stories of their late fathers and Major Shaitan Singh who were friends from school days to the last. I am also thankful to Mr Bhawani Singh, son of late Major Durga Das for sharing an anecdote related to his father and Major Shaitan Singh.

I very much appreciate Mrs Anand Kanwar for the efforts made by her to share the stories of her father the late Lt Col Bijai Singh and Major Shaitan Singh.

I appreciate the efforts made by Mr Digvijay Singh and his son Captain Siddharth Singh (retd) for providing me with information about the Kotah Umed Infantry and late Lt Col Durjan Sal Singh. I am grateful to Mr Mayurdwajh Sinh Parmar for sharing information about his granduncle the late Lt Col Jaswant Sinh Parmar, MBE and Kotah Umed Infantry. I also thank Mr Raghubir Singh Jhala for his inputs about his father the late Major Gulab Singh and Major Shaitan Singh.

I would like to thank Lt Col Daulat Singh (retd), son of the late Lt Col Dungar Singh, MC (JSI) for sharing anecdotes related to Jodhpur State Forces and for the photograph of Major Shaitan Singh with his football team. I'm also thankful to Mr Rajat Singh for providing knowledge on various officers of Jodhpur State Forces.

I also offer my heartiest greetings to Mrs Sagar Kanwar daughter of the late Colonel Rewat Singh for sharing some stories about Major Shaitan Singh.

I am thankful to Mr Haigreev Singh Bhati, grandson of Colonel Mohan Singh, who provided me with information about the Jodhpur State Forces and photographs of his grandfather.

I am obliged to Lt Gen N.K. Singh (retd) who is also a son of Jodhpur Sardar Infantry veteran the late Lt Col Madho Singh for sharing contacts and guiding me throughout the journey. I would also like to thank Mr Deepak Surana and a special thanks to Ms. Shalini Singh Sengar who kept motivating me during the research and writing process. I am also thankful to Mr Jayanta Bhattacharya for his guidance.

I am happy to have friends like Ms Ayushi Tiwari and Mr Yashjeet Bhanwala who helped me meet Brigadier Prem Kumar (retd) and Major Haramrit Singh Dhingra (retd) in Chandigarh. I am thankful to Mr Mohan Singh Naruka who took me to Major Shaitan Singh's college and gave me a wonderful insight of the town of Jodhpur.

Finally, I want to thank my dear friends Suhani Kothari, Ritik Kothari, Akshit Somani, Jonal Jain and all my well wishers and the people who helped me and supported me during this unmatchable journey of researching the life of the great Major Shaitan Singh, PVC.

❑

Contents

Foreword 5

Author's Note 7

Acknowledgements 9

1. Rangadh: The Story of the Brave Father 17

2. Shaitan: The Student—Stories from the School and College Days 27

3. The Making of Shaitan: The Man in the Rajasthan State Forces 39

4. Bedu Pako Baramasa: Days in Six Kumaon 62

5. The Captain: At the Home of Kumaon 85

6. Operation Raji: The Staff Captain 104

7. Major Shaitan Singh: Terah Kumaon 118

8. The Dragon Strikes: The Sino-Indian War of 1962 137

9. The Battle of Chushul 155

10. Aftermath 183

Epilogue 197

End Note 203

Messages 209

Appendix-I 217

Appendix-II 218
Appendix-III 224
Names of Martyrs 226
Abbreviations 230

❑

Rangadh

The Story of the Brave Father

Lt Col Hem Singh, OBI

"The sun rose never to set again"

The initial chapter of the book throws light on the career of Lt Col Hem Singh, OBI, father of Maj Shaitan Singh. It also takes you to the initial years of Jodhpur state forces and Shaitan Singh. It also talks about the family of Shaitan Singh and the story behind his odd name.

The story starts some 133 years ago when a warrior named Hem Singh was born in an ordinary Bhati Rajput family in a village called Banasar situated in the princely state of Jodhpur (now Jodhpur district). Bhati tribes with origins in India claim to be descendants of Krishn (Krishna), an avatar of the Hindu God Vishnu, and thus identify themselves as a Chandravanshi Kshatriya clan. The Bhatis trace their history to the desert regions of Rajasthan's Jaisalmer, in the border villages of Bikaner, and some parts of Jodhpur known as Bhatiana. In addition, Bhati clans are also found in Uttar Pradesh. They are divided into approximately 40 clans.

Hem Singh belonged to the Barsing Bhati Rajput clan of Bhati lineage. He was a son of Aman Singh, a farmer, and his mother was Gulab Kanwar. He was the sixth among the seven brothers. As a child, he couldn't attend school as in those times education was only available to the royal families, nobles, the British, and government bureaucrats. Besides, educational institutions were only available in big towns and cities.

Singh used to help his father in farming, but farming was difficult owing to water scarcity in Jodhpur state. Located in a desert region, it was a famine-prone area. People used to walk for kilometres just to draw drinking water from wells. In those times, farming was the primary source of income and food. Gradually farming became tough due to paucity of water, so most of the Rajput young men joined state forces.

The Sardar Risala

The Rajputs of Marwar had less or no inclination towards infantry. Consequently, it was decided that cavalry should be raised, and two cavalry regiments were raised. Those units were named Sardar Risala after the name of Maharaja Sardar Singh. The organisation of these regiments commenced in 1889 by Sir Pertab/Partap Singh and was completed in 1896.

The Sardar Risala was composed entirely of Rajputs who came from within the territory of Jodhpur state. In 1906, Hem Singh, just 16 years old, with his three brothers went on to get recruited into the Khichi and Bhati Rajput-clan squadron of Sardar Risala.

The men of Sardar Risala were battle-hardened, fond of horses and accustomed to riding. They were sent to various military training centres outside Jodhpur because the state had no local training centre. They were mainly trained for signalling, first aid, and horsemanship.

Hem Singh also learnt to ride horses in various conditions. By training horses for battle-like situations, his skills improved gradually, and he became one of the best equestrians in his regiment. Horse riding was one of his hobbies, but he was also interested in shooting. Organised shooting was not a common sport in those days. However, game hunting was very common. But Hem Singh showed an interest in participation in tournaments and used to train regularly. Days passed and he also became a skilled marksman of his regiment.

The Great War

In 1914 when the First World War started, India was dragged into it. The British Army asked state forces to send their troops to the Great War from their side. Various forces from all over the Indian subcontinent, including the Sardar Risala, agreed to send their troops. On August 28, 1914, the Sardar Risala began their journey for the warfront by a special train to Ahmedabad. From there they proceeded to the war. Three squadrons of the first regiment and one squadron of the second regiment along with their horses were sent to the warfront in France under the leadership of Maj Gen Sir Pertab Singh.

The Jodhpur Sardar Risala arrived in Marseilles on October 12, 1914. They were sent to Orleans where they were to fight the mighty Germans.

The Risala participated in the battle of Ypres and Festubert on October 12, where they lost three men and eight were wounded. They remained on the Western Front for over three years and attempted several times to enter German land. In 1916, the Sardar Risala underwent military training and participated in various battles during the months of July and August. The Germans stood out and the cavalry had to withdraw slightly. The battle continued for several days, but the cavalry was unsuccessful in breaching the German defences.

It was in August, the Germans launched a counterattack and Sardar Risala suffered casualties, including three wounded. Risaldar Hem Singh was among the three wounded. On August 17, 1916 he was shot in his left leg and was severely wounded. He was evacuated to a temporary military hospital where it took him several weeks to recover. In January 1918, the Indian cavalry forces were withdrawn from France, including the Sardar Risala.

From there, the Sardar Risala was sent to Palestine where they fought the legendary Battle of Haifa. Later they were sent to Egypt and then to Aleppo, which is now in Syria. Hem Singh with the Sardar Risala returned to Jodhpur on February 2, 1920, after five years of continuous warfare where tales of the valour of the heroes became the talk of the town and entered folklore.

After the War

When Hem Singh came to Jodhpur after such a long time, his family decided to get him married. He was married to Meera Kanwar of Shergarh, in 1921, but within a few years of his marriage his wife died. The couple didn't have any children. His wife's death made Hem Singh very depressed and sad. This also affected his service life. Therefore, gradually, Hem Singh kept busy in his unit's activities and studies.

Risaldar Major Hem Singh gradually understood the importance of education in life so along with his service he started studying. He put in a lot of hard work. Once in 1922, when there was a vacancy for an officer in Jodhpur Lancers, he applied. Due to his knowledge, experience, and perseverance he was selected and was given the rank of Lieutenant, on November 13, 1922.

In the same year he married again, this time to Jawahar Kanwar of Bethwasiya. From there, Hem Singh did well in his service and family life. On March 15, 1924, he was promoted to the rank of captain. He was sent to various marksmanship competitions of the Army Rifles Association, in which he consistently performed well and won various medals.

The year 1924 was destined to be a good year for Hem Singh. Not only did he get the promotion but was blessed with his first child.

On a usually chilly desert winter day, Jawahar Kanwar gave birth to a boy at their home in Banasar, on December 1, 1924. Hem Singh was elated about the birth of his first child.

As it was Hem Singh's first child, the family arranged a "namkaran" (naming) ceremony at their home. Guests and relatives from the village attended the ceremony. The child was named Udaibhan Singh. "Udaibhan" translates to "rising sun" in English.

Soon after the ceremony, Hem Singh left for Jodhpur to join his unit. A few days later, he was given the task to look after recruitment and training.

In the summer of 1926, Hem Singh's wife and little Udaibhan's mother, Jawahar Kanwar, died of health complications. His second wife's death broke Hem Singh. Udaibhan was too small to understand what had happened. A year passed, Hem Singh's brother Risaldar Sambal Singh who was also part of Jodhpur Lancers and had no child, his wife alone took care of the child.

She raised and took care of Udaibhan and never let him feel the absence of his mother. Hem Singh was anxious about the child so his family suggested that he should think about getting married again.

After thinking about it a lot, Hem Singh decided to marry again – for the third time. In 1928, he married Sire Kanwar of Guda Narkan Ji, which is a village in the Pali district.

Udaibhan's stepmother loved him like her own child. When Udaibhan was four, his sister Chandra Kanwar was born.

Udaibhan was a mischievous child who used to play in his house's courtyard with his young friends from the village. However, Hem Singh knew the importance of education in one's life. He took Udaibhan, who was seven then, to Jodhpur and got the child admitted to the Sumer School, which was a primary school. Udaibhan was a quick learner and a bright student, but he was mischievous as well.

On August 5, 1929, Capt Hem Singh became Maj Hem Singh. With the new rank came a new and an important responsibility. He became the second in command of the same Sardar Risala, which he joined as a sowar in 1906.

A few years later, Maj Hem Singh and Sire Kanwar were blessed with another son who they named Surajbhan Singh – a name synonymous to Udaibhan. Both their names meant the rising sun. A year or two later their second son Lal Singh was born. After the birth of Lal Singh, the couple was blessed with another daughter whom they called Ugam Kanwar, and some years later, around 1936, the youngest son named Prithvi Singh was born.

The Name Shaitan

Once, Udaibhan went with his father to the officers' mess of Jodhpur State Forces. The children of a few other officers were also present. As a child, Udaibhan was an open person. He mingled easily with other children and they started playing and were engaged in mischievous activities. A British Colonel sitting there with Maj Hem Singh looked at little Udaibhan and said the little fellow was "shaitan". When he got to know that he was Hem Singh's son, the colonel suddenly asked Maj Hem Singh to rename Udaibhan Singh as Shaitan Singh. However, Hem Singh was confused by this suggestion of his senior officer because in Urdu, shaitan is a word used for the devil. Although Hem Singh knew Udaibhan was mischievous, he never thought of naming him "Shaitan''. But in those days people used to name their children with odd names because there was a belief that these odd names would protect the children from evil eyes. However, it would have been odd if somebody renamed his child on the suggestion of a senior officer.

Nonetheless, Hem Singh didn't think much because names didn't matter in those times and renamed his first son from Udaibhan Singh to Shaitan Singh.

I was very curious to know the story of how Shaitan Singh got his name because Shaitan is an odd name to give to a child. Now, as we know, this name is now written in golden words in the history of India.

Honours

On June 3, 1935, the British government conferred the Order of British India Class II upon Maj Hem Singh for his selfless service and brave deeds in the Great War. Along with the OBI he was conferred the title of "Bahadur", which means "brave". Maj Hem Singh was also given the rank of honorary lieutenant colonel.

After his retirement in 1935, Hem Singh chose to settle in his village. His main motive to return to his village was to bring some development and education there. Water scarcity was a major problem in his area, so Hem Singh spent his own money digging wells and small water tanks in the village. Since he also knew the importance of education, he sent his own children as well as his brothers' children to school in Jodhpur to get exemplary education. He also made people of his village understand how much education can change the life of an individual and he helped them get their children educated. Hem Singh also did a lot of charity work.

In early 1943, when the Second World War was on, the Jodhpur State Forces expanded in number of personnel. Most of the men who had never been out of the state before now served in a foreign land. The state was worried about their families and relatives who lived in their villages without the news of their family members. The families had to face various difficulties during the absence of those men.

Soon the state realised how major the problem was and, thinking about the welfare of the families, the state approved the creation of the liaison branch at headquarters of Jodhpur State Forces.

Lt Col Shyam Singh was appointed as the chief liaison officer and he had three touring officers under him, including retired Lt Col Hem Singh, Bahadur, OBI of Jodhpur Sardar Risala, who was handpicked for this job.

Hem Singh as a touring officer had duties to tour various villages to make inquiries regarding payments, allowances and letters received and sent by the families, whether the soldiers' families faced any issue, and endeavoured to help them. In general, they had to provide all possible help to the families and relatives of soldiers and then he had to report to the chief liaison officer.

On January 23, 1948 the Maharaja of Jodhpur granted various honours to military personnel on the birth of his son

Maharaja Gaj Singh, Lt Col Hem Singh was awarded the title "Haathi Saropao", permission to wear gold and tazim (The Marwari people continued to remain loyal to their princes who had honoured them with the extremely rare appellation of tazimi-sardar, given to the very select. A tazimi-sardar was allowed to continue sitting in the presence of the Maharaja and allowed to wear gold on his feet, a privilege rarely extended to people outside the immediate circle of the royal family. It used to become a matter of family prestige) for his loyal service to the Jodhpur State.

Maharaja also offered him two villages in Pali (now a district in Rajasthan) to which he refused politely. Through this, he tried to show that bravery and loyalty have no cost, and there is no place for greed in a soldier's life.

References

1. Interview with Mr Narpat Singh s/o Major Shaitan Singh, PVC
2. Interview with Commandant Prithvi Singh (retd) Brother of Major Shaitan Singh, PVC
3. Interview with Mr Mahendra Singh Nephew of Major Shaitan Singh, PVC
4. Service record of Lt Col Hem Singh, OBI (retd)
5. Jodhpur State Forces Record
6. Rajputana and Ajmere Merwara List

❑

Shaitan: The Student

Stories from the School and College Days

Durga Horse Football Team
(L to R) On Ground: Hari Singh, —
On Chairs: —, —, Col Mohan Singh, Randhir Singh, Shaitan Singh
Standing: Nawal Singh, Bhoor Singh, Bahadur Singh, Shivdutt, -

This chapter tells the tales of Shaitan Singh in the Rajput school as a student and his love for the game of football. The chapter focuses on his college life in Jaswant College and also talks about his marriage.

The Rajput School

I went to a school in Jodhpur in November 2019. Its enormous campus is constructed entirely of the renowned red sandstone of Jodhpur. A stunning architectural structure surrounded by low hills and a lake. Located around eight kilometres west of Jodhpur city, it features a lovely plantation around the buildings and very well-maintained playgrounds.

The school has a very rich history dating back to 1875, when two schools were founded. These two schools later merged into one and was named as Powlett Noble School after the British resident Col Powlett. Before Sir Pratap Singh finally established the school in Chopasni in 1914, it was moved to several locations, including Mandore, Jaswantpura, and even the Jalore Fort. On February 8, 1914, the Viceroy of India, Lord Hardinge of Penshurst, originally inaugurated the school, which was called Rajput Elgin School.

The school had five hostels on its large residential campus: Pratap House, Hardinge House, Elgin House, Umaid House, and Powlett House. Powlett House was a special boarding house for wards of noble households, where students received additional amenities and were permitted to hire helpers to assist with daily chores. The hostels included spacious dormitories and enormous dining areas. The school included a sizeable open area with playgrounds for sports, like cricket and football.

The school also offered diverse of extracurricular activities, such as debating, horse riding, gardening, photography, woodworking, and sketching. However, its main emphasis was on the Imperial Cadet Corps, which was designed to prepare cadets for joining the military and state forces.

At that time, Shaitan was attending Sumer School and staying with his father because Jodhpur did not have many other educational options. Despite receiving a primary education there, he was not entirely satisfied. Being an extroverted youngster, he used to feel terribly constrained there.

His father quickly realised that Shaitan felt constrained in his institution. Maj Hem Singh who was now second-in-command of the Sardar Risala had some extra responsibilities being a senior officer. He decided that his son should be transferred to the Rajput School, Chopasni, which was a residential school with various of amenities and activities, and which also housed children of his colleagues and other military officers. He believed Shaitan would get easily adjusted there.

Days in Chopasni

Shaitan was admitted to the first standard at the Rajput School in 1933 after completing his elementary schooling at Sumer School. He was allotted the Pratap House, which, considering that he spent almost 11 years there, was his second home. Chopasni had the advantage of being far from city distractions, and all the staffers and students used to live on campus, which fostered cordial relationships between them and aided in their development.

The school quickly gained a reputation for generating effective military and civilian leaders because of its heritage and culture. Many people who graduated from the school have received honours, and two of its alumni have received the highest gallantry awards of their eras: Maj Shaitan Singh, whose Param Vir Chakra story we have come across, and Lance Daffadar Gobind Singh of the 28th Light Cavalry, who received the Victoria Cross for exhibiting the tremendous bravery and devotion to duty on December 1, 1917, during the Battle of Cambrai.

The school has also produced eminent people like Lt Col Bahadur Singh, OBI a Haifa Hero and both his sons AVM

Chandan Singh, MVC, AVSM, VrC and Brig Hari Singh, AVSM; Lt Col Dungar Singh, MC; Lt Col Mal Singh AC III; and many war heroes are alumni of this acclaimed institution.

Now, returning to the tale of Shaitan Singh from his time in school. His friends recall that he was an enthusiastic learner who always gave studies the top priority. He also developed an interest in football early on, and began to gain fame in Chopasni's sports grounds.

I've heard several anecdotes from his friends and family about his time at school. I wish to share a few.

When Shaitan was in the seventh grade, he changed completely from the child he was when he first arrived at the school and became a quiet and reserved student. Once a new teacher first entered class to teach. He formally introduced himself and requested the students to do the same. Everyone introduced themselves one by one. When it was Shaitan's turn to introduce himself, he stood up and said: "My name is Shaitan."

'You don't seem to be a Shaitan', the teacher said after observing him for a moment as if he was reading him. The entire class broke out in laughter, which made Shaitan feel a shightly awkward. The teacher then silenced the class and prophesied: "Ek din yeh ladka bahut badi shaitani karega aur apna naam siddh karega (One day this boy is going to be invlolved in something memorable and will prove his name)."

I believe the teacher's predictions came true in a very positive light.

Anand Kanwar, the daughter of Shaitan Singh's close friend Lt Col Bijai Singh, has another incident to recount. She says that her father used to share certain recollections with her about his time in Chopasni's school. He consistently emphasised that Shaitan was very sincere about his studies and that he never skipped class, not even for football.

Of all the tales, the one about how some schoolmates or groups would sneak out of the hostel at night to go boar hunting in the adjacent fields caught my attention. After a successful hunt, the boys would return to their hostels, hide the dead boar, and afterwards cook it. However, this didn't always happen. Different groups would occasionally steal the boar, cook it whole, and consume it. The boar thieves were the most wanted individuals. This often caused a furore inside the hostel.

One fine day, someone observed that several of the wards had digestive issues, and it became a pattern after practically every boar hunt. Because boar meat is incredibly hard to digest and can result in indigestion, the hunters used to catch the group who had stolen the boar the next day by looking into who those experiencing digestive issues. To catch boar thieves in the hostel, this became standard procedure. Even though Shaitan Singh was a vegetarian and never hunted, I felt compelled to share this fascinating tale about the hostel where he once resided.

Maj Gen Kishan Singh, AVSM, recalls his father, who was a classmate of Maj Shaitan Singh, telling him about Shaitan Singh being a very sincere student who always focused on studies and being a very skilled footballer. Kishan Singh is the son of Brig Hari Singh, AVSM. Although students at Chopasni School were taught how to swim and had access to a good swimming pool, some of his father's associates would slip out of class and go to the nearby Filter House to swim in the Kailana lake and cause trouble.

In Chopasni, football fever was never low. The best footballers in Marwar state came from this place. The school club used to compete in several competitions throughout the year. The All-India Labhshankar Football Challenge Cup was one of the national-level competitions where the team used to compete, and many of the players trained for it. At the school level, there were appropriate selection processes for the competition. When I visited the Chopasni School, I was told Shaitan Singh was considered as one of the greatest football players ever to grace these school grounds, and he never missed a football match. In 1942, Shaitan Singh was chosen for the team that would represent Chopasni at the national level. He participated in the All-India Labhshankar Football Challenge Cup, where his team finished second overall in India. At the time, Shaitan was a student in the tenth grade. Even though they came in second, the school's principal, A.P. Coxx, was very pleased with him.

Shaitan Singh continued to practise and polish his football skills as well as represent his school in many more events before leaving the school in 1943, after passing the matriculation exam. He was one of the 20 students out of 30 in his class who passed the exams and received a second division.

Many students in Chopasni, including Shaitan and his many classmates, were military officers' wards. The Imperial Cadet Corps had a beneficial influence on students in Chopasni and served as a feeder for the state forces. After graduating from high school, most of Shaitan's acquaintances, including Chandan Singh, Hari Singh, Rewat Singh of Dakha, and Mal Singh enlisted in the Jodhpur State Forces. Bijay Singh became a jailor at the state jail. Due to a limitation of vacancies in the Jodhpur state, Shaitan Singh's seniors Shivji Singh, Bhairon Singh, Sangram Singh, Veer Singh, and Pratap Singh joined the state forces of Kotah.

Shaitan Gets Married

Shaitan was raised in a Rajput military-oriented family. Because his father was an officer in the Jodhpur Lancers, he had grown up surrounded by military practices. Shaitan had experienced the early death of his mother, Jawahar Kanwar. His stepmother Ugam Kanwar raised him. He was the oldest of the family's six children. Surajbhan Singh, Shaitan's younger brother, was close to him. Shaitan was a highly devoted member of the family despite attending a boarding school since he was a small child and spending limited time with them. From the school hostel, he sent frequent letters to his family.

Commandant Prithvi Singh recalls his brother's marriage and how kind and modest he was. He was always respectful of his elders and never raised his voice. He says Lt Col Hem Singh arrived in the summer of 1943 while on leave from Jodhpur. He got off the train at Amla station, which was a few miles away from Banasar and required a walk or a camel cart ride to get there. He additionally states that while his father travelled home on a cart and in the sweltering desert heat, he noticed a girl carrying water containers to her home. The girl received inquiries by Hem Singh about her family, but she shyly walked without responding.

After Hem Singh arrived at his house, he later asked about the girl's family. He discovered that she was Sugan Kanwar, daughter of Amla villager Jagmal Singh. Hem Singh saw Jagmal Singh in Amla the following day and informed him of the earlier event. As early marriage was a normal practice in those days, he further proposed that he would like his son Shaitan to marry Sugan. The family of Shri Jagmal Singh gladly agreed to this.

Shaitan, who was in Jodhpur and had just completed his schooling, was unaware of this. Shaitan was called to his village a few days later, where his father informed him of the marriage proposal. The family went to Amla the following day to conduct the pre-wedding rituals after Shaitan extended his approval. The day of the wedding was likewise set for July.

Sugan Kanwar and Shaitan tied the knot on July 10, 1943. The dowry system was widely used in those days, but Hem Singh broke with tradition and paid for all the expenses incurred on both the groom's and the bride's sides. Shaitan's loved ones and friends came to the very simple ceremony.

Shaitan returned to Jodhpur a month after his wedding, this time to apply for admission to a college where he could earn his graduation degree. He wrote letters to his wife and family from his hostel in Jodhpur. During his winter break from college, he also went to see them.

Shaitan and Sugan Kanwar welcomed a boy into the world, on October 15, 1944, who they called Narpat. Narpat meant a king or emperor. Shaitan was in the first year of his degree programme and resided in a hostel when Narpat was born.

Move to become a Barrister

Shaitan passed his school exams, with a hope of studying law. He had developed a keen interest in higher studies and lacked the desire to join the military. He enrolled in the Jaswant College in 1943. In the same year, the college was completing its 50 years of establishment. The Jaswant College was founded by Maharaja Sir Pratap Singh on August 14, 1893. The college was initially at the intermediate level and was affiliated with Allahabad University. The college was named after Maharaja Jaswant Singh ji Sahib Bahadur. The institution was a boon from the Maharaja to the people of Jodhpur as it gave them access to higher education.

After the intermediate college's satisfactory examination results, its status was elevated to that of a degree college in 1896, and courses for a BA degree commenced. In the initial years of its establishment, the college suffered as the passing rates dropped due to the unpopularity of higher education in those days. Getting the students to take an informed interest in their work rather than merely studying for exams at the end of the semester was the main challenge. Low matriculation standards meant that new college students had weak English language skills and struggled to pay attention in class.

The college's most significant phase of growth was between 1942 and 1943, which helped it become a full-fledged degree-granting institution with faculties of the arts, sciences, and commerce. In response to the overwhelming demand for admissions, the government authorised the expansion of teaching staff and approved the availability of 60 seats in place of the previous 40 in each class.

In 1943, the college broke its previous record, which was seen as the pinnacle year for the institution in terms of the accomplishments of the students in terms of both sports and exams.

Later years saw a continuation of the college's honourable and exemplary traditions. With a 91.8 per cent pass rate in the 1945 BA examinations, the college ranked top among all the colleges of the university in terms of merit. Along with its successes in exams and sports, character-building activities like volunteer labour were rigorously maintained.

Due to the overwhelming number of applicants, the government was happy to increase the class size cap to 60 students in each class, starting from July 1942, and to recruit additional employees. The government also approved the beginning of B.Sc. and B.Com. classes in July 1943 as more students completed the intermediate science and commerce examinations. Both actions provided the parents, guardians, and students with the long-needed relief.

Shaitan enrolled for the Arts department. He selected Hindi, Economics, and History in his first year of arts. He also availed accommodation in the college hostel, which was required for his B.A. studies. The college had two hostels. Sixty-four students were housed in the hostels in 1942. This number rose to 75 in 1943 and 80 in 1944. Owing to a lack of space, some students could not be accommodated in the hostels. In July 1945, a third hostel in Sardarpura opened its doors to 17 students. The other two hostels, which could accommodate 48 and 32 students, were constantly occupied.

The arts faculty contained four large classrooms as well as the vice-principal's office, which was in the same block. The arts faculty was separated into several departments. There was a history department supervised by Hem Raj Gopal Ram and helped by Deo Raj Upadhyaya. DN Bhargava oversaw the English department, which was one of the college's most important and largest in terms of strength. He was aided by Ramakant Tripathi, Gopal Krishna Vyas, and P.N. Shrivastava. Somnath Gupta headed the Hindi department, while W.V. Wadhwani, the vice-principal, directed the economics department, which was assisted by Noor Mohammad Qureshi. The faculty's physical education instructor was Mohan Lal Sharma, a former football player of distinction who also trained students for a variety of sports and prepared sports teams for various tournaments. Shaitan also trained under him.

There weren't many students who chose to study mathematics because it was an unpopular subject. The most popular subject was economics, so Shaitan also chose to study economics.

The structure of tutorial classes in addition to class lectures helped students overcome these challenges. To guide their studies and ensure that they worked methodically, readers met their students late at night. Essay writing, class discussions, and library reading received additional focus to improve English.

To enhance the students' generally poor physique, mandatory games were also made a part of the college schedule. Many pupils were still extremely lethargic and terrible at games. The college had a strong football team, and Shaitan played for them. They reached the Rogers Tournament semifinals and twice tied Rajput School teams in the Marwar Football League, which was founded in 1927 to promote students' participation in sports and physical development in schools and colleges. There were two divisions in the football event. The Rajput High School won the challenge cup in the senior division, with the college coming in second. This was a significant advancement from their earlier performances.

Shaitan attended college for four years total, including one year for an intermediate F.A. (First Year Arts) and three years for a degree. He participated consistently in collegiate co-curricular activities and athletic competitions. His favourite sports were football and horse riding. He appeared for the university exams in July 1947, passed them with a third-division score, and on November 8, 1947, received his Bachelor of Arts degree.

References

1. Interview with Colonel Shivji Singh (retd)
2. Interview with Mr Narpat Singh s/o Maj Shaitan Singh, PVC
3. Interview with Mrs Anand Kanwar d/o Lt Col Bijai Singh
4. Interview with Mr Sajjan Singh s/o AVM Chandan Singh, MVC, AVSM, VrC
5. Telephonic interview with Maj Gen Kishan Singh (retd) s/o Brig Hari Singh, AVSM
6. Centenary celebration book of Chopasni School
7. Golden Jubilee celebration book of Jaswant College
8. School and College Degrees of Major Shaitan Singh

❑

The Making of Shaitan

The Man in the Rajasthan State Forces

Lt Shaitan Singh, Kotah Umed Infantry

This chapter focuses on how Major Shaitan Singh changed his mind and joined the Jodhpur state forces instead of becoming a barrister and later trained for the Indian Army and went to Dras as a commissioned officer in the Kotah Umed Infantry. The chapter also talks about the merger of state forces and transfers of Shaitan Singh.

Jodhpur was the largest independent princely state in Rajasthan and had its own government and administration when India got its freedom in 1947. Despite having a Rajput king and a sizeable Hindu population, the princely state oddly leaned towards Pakistan.

Hanvant Singh, a youthful and inexperienced prince from Jodhpur, believed that because his state bordered Pakistan, he might be able to negotiate a better "deal" with Islamabad. According to reports, Jinnah gave the Maharaja a signed blank sheet of paper on which to enumerate all his requests. As the Jodhpur state kept a well-organised state force, including units of the Jodhpur Lancers and Jodhpur Sardar Infantry, he also gave him free access to the Karachi port for the manufacturing and importation of weapons with military and agrarian support.

As soon as Sardar Patel realised the dangers of the border princely state joining Pakistan, he called the prince and made an adequate offer. Patel reassured him that importing weapons would be permitted, that Jodhpur and Kathiawar would be connected by train, and that India would provide goods to it in times of famine. Patel's arguments prevailed and the Jodhpur state was added to the Indian dominion, on August 11, 1947, when Maharaja Hanvant Singh, Jodhpur's king, signed the instrument of accession.

Shaitan took his university exams at the same time as India gained its freedom. He expected to receive his results by November. He planned to apply for additional legal education since his goal was to pursue a career as a lawyer.

The Durga Horse

Shaitan played football matches in Jodhpur while he awaited the outcome of his university exams. While playing one of these games with the Royal Bodyguard (Durga Horse). Col Mohan Singh, the commandant of the Durga Horse and a member of the Jodhpur royal family, was also present there. Mohan Singh as a state officer cadet in the Jodhpur Lancers had served under Shaitan's father, Hem Singh. He saw Shaitan while playing and met him after the game to have a life-changing conversation with him.

The conversation went something like this:

Col Mohan Singh: Are you Shaitan Singh, the eldest son of Lt Col Hem Singh?

Shaitan: Yes, Sir

Col Mohan Singh: I saw you playing the game, you're a good footballer. I really appreciate your game.

Shaitan: Thank you, Sir. If I'm not mistaken, you are Col Mohan Singh. I have known you since childhood when my father was in the Lancers.

Col Mohan Singh: Oh! is that so? I've served under your father. He used to be the second in command of the Lancers when I was a state officer cadet. Well, what do you want to do in your future? Are you planning to join the forces and become an officer like your father?

Shaitan: No, Sir, I've recently appeared for the university exams and am waiting for my results so that I can seek admission in a law school. I want to become a lawyer.

Col Mohan Singh: Son, you want to become a lawyer, it's surprising. You seem to be a good sportsman and a well-read man. In my opinion you should join the forces.

Shaitan: Sir, I've never thought of joining the forces. I feel that I'm not made for the forces. I've always wanted to become a lawyer, that's why I completed my graduation. Else, I would have joined the forces just after completing school.

Col Mohan Singh: Son, your father, I've served under him. He is a great man. You should continue his legacy. I see a soldier in you. You must join the forces; you will certainly do well. I will ask you to join my unit, Durga Horse.

Shaitan: All right, Sir, I will think about it because it's a totally different profession from what I want to be.

Col Mohan Singh: Son, take your time, and let me assure you that you won't regret joining the forces. It's a better career for you than becoming a lawyer.

The Cavalier

Shaitan met Col Mohan Singh at Durga Horse a few days later, in the last week of October 1947. Shaitan told Mohan Singh: "Sir, I considered your proposal and discussed it with my father as well. I am prepared to enlist in the military." In his reply, a happy Mohan Singh said, "Son, meet me on Sunday. You will be recruited as a state officer candidate in my regiment, Durga Horse (Jodhpur Bodyguard), following some formalities and physical examinations.

Shaitan met Col Mohan Singh in the early hours of November 2, which was a Sunday. (Coincidentally, Shaitan's military career started on a Sunday and ended on a Sunday, and that too in November.) Shaitan, who was a sportsman, performed well during the physical exam and the formalities were a breeze. On that day, he was made a state officer cadet in the Durga Horse.

To preserve the heritage of the horse-mounted cavalry when the Jodhpur Lancers were mechanised, a new unit was raised in Jodhpur. I would like the readers to be aware of the Durga Horse story.

When Maharaja Umaid Singh learned that the commander-in-chief had chosen the Jodhpur Lancers for mechanisation, the first Indian state unit to be chosen for mechanisation, this news came as a complete surprise to him. He immediately accepted it as an honour for the regiment and the state.

The Durga Horse, formerly known as Jodhpur Bodyguard Squadron, was raised in February 1941.

There was certainly some sadness and regret as the regiment would lose its cherished horses. However, it meant that the regiment would undergo modernisation and have a greater chance of being sent on active duty abroad. The Rajputs of Jodhpur state are very passionate about horse-related sports, including equestrian, polo, pig sticking, tent-pegging, jumping, and so on. The Jodhpur Lancers' horses belonged to the state, and the regiment had a reputation for being one of India's finest mounted cavalry units, thanks to its participation in the Great War.

The fact that the regimental horses would be replaced by tanks or armoured cars, therefore, caused tremendous concern among many people in the state as well as the Maharaja and the officers of the regiment. It and it was felt that something urgently needed to be done to keep at least some of the regiment's horses.

At that point, the Maharaja gave his approval to the concept of a horse-mounted bodyguard squadron.

To possibly return some of the regimental horses from Risalpur where the Jodhpur Lancers were posted to Jodhpur for the bodyguard squadron, which was about to be formed, Brigadier R.C. Duncan, the commandant of the Jodhpur State Forces, travelled to Delhi with the objective of returning, if possible, some of the regimental horses from Risalpur to Jodhpur. The request was met with great favour by the officials in Delhi, who not only consented to the return of 350 horses from the regiment to the state but also succeeded in getting the Indian government to foot the bill for their train transportation from Risalpur to Jodhpur.

These horses were selected by a committee of Jodhpur Lancers officers, and the finest horses in the regiment, almost all the polo horses were sent to Jodhpur.

Of these 350 horses, 200 were for the Jodhpur Bodyguard Squadron, and the other 150 were sold at a discount to state-approved buyers with the caveat that they could be called up at any moment, if necessary.

Maharaja Umaid Singh instructed Brig R.C. Duncan to raise the Jodhpur Bodyguard Squadron as a state service unit in May 1941. It consisted of three troops of Rajputs, and one troop of Kayamkhanis.

Capt Mangal Singh of the Jodhpur Lancers Training Centre was named the commandant and Lt Achal Singh was chosen as the adjutant and quartermaster. Lt Achal Singh had extensive knowledge of the duties and instruction of a bodyguard unit because he had served as the Bengal Bodyguard's commander for the six months before his return to Jodhpur.

The Jodhpur Bodyguard Squadron was authorised to have two state officers, four Indian officers (JCOs and NCOs), 125 Indian other ranks, ninety non-combatants (enrolled), and 180 horses.

A limited number of pensioners from Indian Cavalry regiments, like the 2nd Royal Lancers, 16th Cavalry, Poona Horse, and 18th KEO Cavalry, comprised the squadron's personnel, which was primarily made up of pensioners or men who had been discharged from the Jodhpur Sardar Risala. Many of the men of the squadron were veterans of the First World War.

The Jodhpur Bodyguard Squadron was fully operational and expertly equipped in less than three months. In a freshly formed unit, there is always a lot to plan and organise as well as many challenges to overcome. However, Capt Mangal Singh and Lt Achal Singh handled arrangements brilliantly, and the squadron quickly assumed its duties as the Palace Guard.

The expensive horses of the regimental polo ride were well-cared for, trained, and frequently used in polo matches.

After leading the Jodhpur Bodyguard Squadron for two and a half years, Capt Mangal Singh retired on pension and was given the position of commander of the Fort Guard. Lt Achal Singh, who on November 16, 1943, was promoted as captain, took over as its commandant.

On October 25, 1945, it was renamed Jodhpur Bodyguard, and on December 12, 1946, it underwent another name change to become Durga Horse in honour of Veer Durga Das, a Rathore Rajput general in the Marwar. Following the death of Maharaja Jaswant Singh in the seventeenth century, he is recognised for safeguarding the Rathore dynasty's rule over Marwar. He had to stand up to Aurangzeb and engage the Mughals in several conflicts to accomplish this.

In the same year, Col Mohan Singh of Jodhpur Lancers assumed command of the Durga Horse. The Durga Horse had demonstrated that it was not only a decorative component of the Jodhpur State Forces but also a functional unit with active duties in the state.

In Durga Horse, Shaitan already had Hari Singh, a classmate and Durga Das from Jaipur state, who were also state officer cadets.

Both Shaitan and Hari Singh were reputed football players in town. The Durga Horse Mess, an opulent two-storey structure with an indoor pool on the ground floor, used to be where the cadets resided. These cadets and their helpers had access to the full building. Governmental institutions are now housed in the structure.

The best athletes from Durga Horse competed in regional and national competitions as well as equestrian events.

Previously, the Marwar state hosted the Marwar Football League Tournament. Several Marwar state teams, including teams from the Jodhpur State Forces, competed in the competition. The Durga Horse team won the Marwar Football League in 1948 and received the trophy and shield that were traditionally given to the winning club by the reigning champions. When the competition ceased to exist in 1949, the Jodhpur Sardar Infantry was the last to take home the trophy and shield.

The Durga Horse was used for more than just ceremonial purposes; in addition to serving as guard for the Jodhpur Palace, it was also frequently called upon during citywide disturbances, during which it performed its responsibilities most successfully.

Shaitan served in the unit for nearly one and a half years in 1949, but he continued to be a State Officer Cadet in the Durga Horse due to a state force provision which states that only the state officer cadet will be promoted to the rank of Lieutenant and receive a commission from the state if there is a vacancy at the officer level. Otherwise, they continued serving as officer cadets.

The Kachhawa Horse of the Jaipur State Forces was combined with the Durga Horse and a portion of the Jodhpur Lancers of the Jodhpur State Forces, along with the Dungar Lancers of the Bikaner State Forces, Mangal Lancers of the Alwar State Forces, and Mewar Lancers of the Mewar State Forces, to form an amalgamated horse cavalry unit in May 1949. Later, in 1954, when the-then prime minister, Jawaharlal Nehru, wrote to the-then defence minister, Krishna Menon, that "India must preserve a horsed cavalry regiment which shall serve as a link between the past and the present," the Jodhpur/Kachhawa Horse was amalgamated with a few other horse cavalry units, including the Gwalior Lancers, the Rajendra Lancers, and the Mysore Lancers, to raise the 61st Cavalry.

Shaitan Trains for the Indian Army

All the units which were merged sent their cadets to Jaipur, where the Rajasthan State Forces Headquarters was situated. The cadets were required to remain there for a month and a half and take promotional tests to be evaluated and chosen to be sent to different officers' training schools. Most of the cadets of the Jodhpur Brigade (formation of units of Jodhpur State Forces), including Shaitan and a few of his friends were sent to the Officer Training School, Poona.

Now, Shaitan travelled outside Rajasthan for the first time in his life.

Shaitan was instructed to arrive in Poona by July 23 to make it in time for the course to start on July 25 at one of the nation's oldest institutions, Deccan College, where the training facility was situated.

His call letter advised him to take a second-class train ticket. However, he took a first-class ticket and arrived in Poona on July 24 instead, which was his first offence even before arriving at the OTS. Shaitan arrived on the 24th, so he had to manage everything on his own. The OTS had provided transportation services to transport the cadets to the establishment on July 23.

He reported his arrival to the adjutant at Deccan College, where he was given accommodation and undoubtedly received some sort of punishment for arriving late at the school.

The first day of the training was Monday, July 25. The cadets were informed of the demanding timetable they would have at school. There was arduous physical training as well as academic warfare studies courses.

During the training, Shaitan was joined by his high school friend Bijai Singh, as well as Moti Singh and Mod Singh from Jodhpur.

Sporting events and other pursuits were also required of the cadets. Being a football player, Shaitan played the game and made some acquaintances there, including Pratap Singh who belonged to the Bikaner State Forces

After only a week at the OTS, Shaitan got his commission into the Army, on August 1, which changed his rank from officer cadet to second lieutenant.

On September 2, 1949, the supplementary course ended after 40 days of training. Shaitan's military career in the Indian Army officially began when the passing out parade took place on the morning of September 3, 1949.

He travelled to Jodhpur with other officers from the Jodhpur Brigade for a brief leave and to complete the necessary paperwork for their new postings. The transfers and welfare of the soldiers and officers of the Rajasthan State Forces were handled by the Rajasthan State Forces Headquarters in Jaipur. The Headquarters in October assigned Shaitan to the Kotah Umed Infantry at Dras.

From Desert to Dras

On October 8, 1949, a chilly Saturday in Dras, no snow had yet begun to fall. In the late afternoon, when the temperature was three-degrees celsius, a convoy carrying soldiers and supplies from Srinagar arrived. A young man who experienced this type of cold for the first time just came from a short break after his training and commissioning. He was approached by a soldier after descending from a truck with a question.

"I want to meet Capt Shivji Singh, where is he?" the officer asked. "Major Sahab is on the post, what happened?" the soldier replied.

The young man introduced himself as a newly commissioned officer assigned to this unit and a friend of Maj Shivji. Saluting the young officer, the soldier said, "Sahabji, I'll take you to Maj Gulab Singh."

The soldier accompanied the subaltern to a small tin hut to meet Maj Gulab Singh. "Sahab, someone has come to meet you," the soldier informed. "Send him in," the major said. The new subaltern entered, saluted Maj Gulab, and introduced himself as 2/Lt Shaitan Singh, SF-GR No. 321 (State Forces Greater Rajasthan) and said, "Sir, I'm a native of Jodhpur. I'm a friend of Maj Shivji Singh, I was his school and college junior."

Maj Gulab greeted the officer by saying, "Welcome brother to Kotah. Well, Capt Shivji is now Major Shivji and is on his post right now. He'll come down tomorrow, then you can meet him."

(You must be curious as to how one would say "welcome to Kotah" in Dras. So let me tell you about the story behind it.

The Kotah Umed Infantry, which was originally raised as Govardhan Paltan in the eighteenth century, is what is indicated by the term "Kotah". It was re-raised in November 1929 under the Indian State Forces scheme by Col Prithvi Singh, MBE, the GOC of Kotah State Forces. Rajputs and Gujars made up most of the unit's strength, but there were also some Gurkhas, Muslims, and Minas.

The unit relocated to Lahore during the Second World War. In 1941, after being upgraded to full battalion, it was sent to the Punjab and eventually to Sindh. It participated in the Hur Operations in 1943 before moving to Drigh Road for airfield defence responsibilities later in the same year. In January 1944 unit's officer Maj Jaswant Sinh was awarded the MBE. On August 16, 1944 the battalion left India for service in Iraq, Persia, Egypt, and Syria, where it was a part of the 24th Indian Infantry Brigade. It returned to India on May 13, 1946.

The battalion was stationed in Gurdaspur in Punjab during the first India-Pakistan war (1947–1948). While two companies were attached to the 4th Battalion, 11th Gorkha Rifles (now disbanded), in the Dera Baba Nanak area, for the defence of a strategic bridge there. The Paltan relocated to the Jammu & Kashmir Theatre in Dras in early 1949 where it belonged to the now-disbanded 77 Para Brigade).

Shaitan was escorted by a soldier to the officer's accommodations following a brief meeting with Maj Gulab. As Dras is the coldest inhabited region in India and is located at an elevation of around 11,000 feet above sea level, it was advised that he should rest and acclimatise himself.

The next day Maj Shivji came down from his post and was informed that 2/Lt Shaitan Singh had joined the unit. Shivji was pleased to hear that as they were both from Jodhpur, and he was his school and college senior and also a good friend. Both their fathers, Lt Col Hem Singh and Major Sardar Singh, also served together in the same regiment of Jodhpur State Forces.

Maj Shivji went to meet Shaitan and knocked on his door. Opening the gate, Shaitan gave Shivji an ecstatic hug. After exchanging notes for a while about Jodhpur and recalling their school days, Maj Shivji gave Shaitan a briefing on the Kotah Umed Infantry and the surrounding area because Shaitan was now a member of the unit as well. He also explained to Shaitan the crucial part the unit plays in patrolling. Shaitan was also informed by Maj Shivji that there was a vacancy in his company. He added, "I'll ask the CO and adjutant if they can assign you to my company, but there's a vacancy for IO in the unit. Maybe, the CO can also name you as the Intelligence Officer or IO."

Shaitan was asked to meet the CO that day in the afternoon. The CO, Lt Col Durjan Sal Singh, a kind and skilled officer from Dabri, Kotah. The CO gave Shaitan a warm greeting, he enquired about his health as well as his training and prior military experience. "Shaitan, I don't know how much you know about this paltan, but always remember "Veer Bhogya Vasundhara" is our paltan's motto. Perform your duties with passion and dedication. You'll achieve the greatest one day, I wish you the best," the CO added.

Shaitan was invited to the mess in the afternoon for lunch, where he met Capt Pratap Singh, Maj Veer Singh, Maj Sangram Singh all of whom were from the Marwar or Jodhpur state, and the second in command, Maj Ranjit Singh of Palaitha. They all welcomed Shaitan in the unit and had some casual conversation about their home state and about the unit's drill and operations.

The CO and the adjutant agreed without reluctance to assign Shaitan to Maj Shivji's company the following day.

Life in 40 Pound Tents

Shaitan joined the company, which was a few kilometres from the battalion headquarters, in the early morning of Wednesday, October 12. He was welcomed to a post of B company by the JCOs, NCOs, and ORs after being introduced to them. A 40-pound officer's tent was allotted to him, whereas soldiers lived in 180-pound tents. There was a paucity of suitable winter clothing and supplies.

The battalion was stretched for about 30 miles along the ceasefire line, manning tiny pockets and picquets at elevations ranging from 13,000 to 14,000 feet. A single company was responsible for safeguarding nearly 10 miles of frontage. There were numerous incidents of ceasefire violations. The advantage of being at such heights was having an aerial view for broad observation. Since the attackers would be vulnerable to direct fire, the goal was to dominate the hill tops.

Soon, after a period of five days, CO Lt Col Durjan Sal was transferred to command the subarea Kotah and later the Mewar Bhil Corps in Kherwara, near Udaipur. The Kotah Umed Infantry now had Lt Col Jaswant Sinh J. Parmar, MBE as its commanding officer. He was commissioned into the Dhrangadhra Makhwan

Infantry in 1924 and was a very honourable officer. From 1937 till 1941, he commanded the Makhwan Infantry before moving to the Kotah Umed Infantry during the Second World War as the Dhrangadhra Makhwan Infantry was disbanded. He received the Member of the Order of the British Empire on January 1, 1944, for his meritorious contributions while serving with the Kotah Umed Infantry. Now, he finally returned to lead the unit. He was a disciplined, tough, and well-trained officer who was also known to be a hard task master.

Shaitan was soon assigned to conduct a patrol the very next day. The purpose of the patrol was to explain the topography and strategic significance of the area to Shaitan. It was a short-range patrol that was believed to be a routine activity in the unit, and an experienced JCO and 10 ORs were sent on the patrol. A few months earlier, the war operations had come to an end, but there were ceasefire violations. There were still high chances that the enemy might assault or seize a post nearby.

Because of this, the region was regularly patrolled. Shaitan's patrol carried supplies, weapons, maps, and binoculars. The patrol reached the company base 30 hours after finishing the assignment. Shaitan had never taken part in a patrol like this. He learnt several lessons from it and acquired plenty of knowledge about the geography of the sector.

After a few days, on October 30, Shaitan was named the Kotah Umed Infantry's intelligence officer. Working with the CO to handle maps and strategies was part of his job as an IO.

Shaitan wrote letters to his family, he always cared for their needs and asked his brothers about their studies. He was always anxious about his father's health.

Soon winter arrived. Winters in Dras are incredibly dangerous and bone-chilling. Troops from both sides began to vacate their posts and began their journey down where they had to stay till March. The soldiers of Kotah Umed Infantry were instructed to pull back from hilltop positions momentarily but keep an eye on the enemy, who might seize any post in the area.

Range Takers Course

Shaitan was sent to Mhow in December 1949 for the range-takers course, which is a course for learning how to operate heavy and medium machine guns (HMG and MMG). In the course, he performed excellently and scored well.

The Winters of Dras

It snowed heavily when he returned from the course. In the month of January, the temperature might drop as low as –20°C. The patrolling groups frequently went on patrols because the snow factor increased the likelihood that the enemy could infiltrate and capture any post. On them, winters were also quite harsh. The same applied to the terrain. The patrolling groups were instructed to move in the mornings as it was considered that the sun's heat at the time of dawn would not be strong enough to melt snow and cause avalanches and it was also common to face bitter cold winds at midday. Weather was very unpredictable as it used to snow on one hilltop and the other had bright sunshine.

The patrol parties would go to Point 5062 and Tololing, and occasionally even to Point 5353 close to the enemy post. The speed of the troops was slower than what it used to be before the winter. Snowfall made things more difficult, marching troops always found themselves knee deep in the snow. Safety precautions were the priority as there was an immense danger of avalanches. There was also an increase in the number of casualties mostly by the effects of such harsh winters.

Maj Shivji Singh, now a retired colonel and a centenarian, recalls how Shaitan and he used to go on long-range patrols, and as an IO, Shaitan occasionally could not match the timeline and had to receive reprimands from the CO but never felt bad for it.

Shaitan had additional work for both the unit and the company. He was always willing to learn from his mistakes and try harder the next time. He was an absolute leader of his men; and was admired by his troops.

Man-management was extremely challenging at such a high altitude, troops were isolated, and there was no source of recreation. The picquets were so remote that there was no human settlement nearby. The company and battalion headquarters were also located far from such posts. It took weeks for letters to arrive. Shaitan accepted the situation tried to solve the issue. Finally he was able to obtain a deck of cards for his platoon and encouraged troops to engage in recreational activities. Because outdoor games were out of the question, the men played cards and other indoor games. He looked after his troops well, and by the end of February, he was asked to hand over the command of the platoon to the JCO and return to battalion base. It took him 12 hours to reach the battalion headquarters. The CO asked him about the state of his platoon's position and any recent enemy activity when they met the next day. Shaitan assured his CO that his troops were in fine condition and that there were no reports of hostile activity.

Unit Education Course

Shaitan was sent to Pachmarhi on March 1 for a month-long unit education officer's course. He completed the course successfully. After that, Shaitan was given approval for his first annual leave. From Pachmarhi he took a bus to Bhopal and from there, he boarded a train to Jodhpur. He was overjoyed to arrive at Jodhpur and rushed to see his brother-in-law (his sister's husband), Mool Singh. A significant supporter throughout his life, Mool Singh and he had a close relationship.

Mool Singh asked Shaitan about his posting and the environment of the unit. To which Shaitan replied that Shivji was there and he was fortunate to be in his company. He added that he was also the IO of the unit, and everything was going well. After a conversation over tea, they went to sleep.

The following day, Shaitan travelled home by train from Jodhpur. They had to use camel carts to get home because the railway station was several kilometres away from his house. Everyone was joyful and eager to welcome him home when he arrived. At home, Shaitan assisted his brothers with their studying and official processes and took care of his sick father. He assisted his wife Sugan Kanwar in getting water from nearby water sources because he was aware that it was summer and getting water in the desert was a most challenging task.

For a few days he went to Jodhpur for some official work and to meet his friends. Colonel Mohan Singh was the first person he went to see. When he arrived at his house, Colonel Mohan Singh gave him a warm welcome and inquired about his health. They discussed Shaitan's posting and his family.

Shaitan also met his friends Bijai Singh and Hari Singh, who were now serving in the Lt Col Dungar Singh, MC-commanded Jodhpur Sardar Infantry. They discussed their service experiences and reminisced about their time spent together. The trio had a solid reputation in football and had played the game frequently together. They had represented Jodhpur on a national level.

Time to Go Back

Shaitan returned home after this, and his leave ended after a week. Everyone wished him the best. His family members were dismayed when he left, and Shaitan promised to return as soon as possible. He left his home and took a train to Jodhpur, where he changed trains to get to Srinagar. On May 14 he returned to the unit's location. The two countries' relations improved slightly, and the weather too got better.

Patrolling was now easier as the snow started to melt. But the CO was neither happy nor satisfied. "We were always prepared for conflict", he reportedly said, 'but the government never gave us orders to advance.' Patrolling and other exercises occupied the months.

When August arrived, the Kotah Umed Infantry arrived in Srinagar in the same month from Dras. The 77 Para Brigade commander Brig GIS Kullar and the GOC of the Baramulla-based 19 Infantry Division, Maj Gen Mahadeo Singh, DSO paid a visit to the battalion in the middle of August. They enquired about the soldiers' and officers' experiences in the high-altitude posting.

Amalgamation of Kotah

Before relocating to Alwar in October 1950, the battalion worked in Srinagar for one month performing administrative tasks. It is stated that there were some disturbances after Independence. Therefore the unit was relocated to Alwar to maintain the peace. Shaitan was still the unit's IO and continued to be in Maj Shivji's company. The company oversaw the security of an important ammunition dump. Soon after the tension in Alwar was brought under control the unit was moved to Bikaner, where a few other state forces units were also located.

As a result of the screening of personnel by selection boards and the decision to reduce the strength of the army by 50,000 during 1951, it was impossible to retain all the units of the old state forces. According to news reports that December, the units were either to be disbanded or amalgamated with Indian Army units. Soldiers could apply to the Indian Army if they wanted to volunteer. The unit worked for the following three months to train the volunteers so they could join the Indian Army.

The administration of the unit began planning the transfer of soldiers and officers as well as the disbandment and merge in March 1951.

The Kotah Umed Infantry ceased to exist on March 31, 1951. In Rajasthan, the number of men who had been declared fit for absorption could make only four infantry units. Together with volunteers from Alwar Jey Paltan, Bharatpur Infantry, volunteers from Kotah were transferred to the Mewar Bhupal Infantry and formed the Mewar Infantry, which was given affiliation with the Rajputana Rifles before being absorbed into the Grenadiers Regiment in 1954. There, it was designated as the 9th Battalion the Grenadiers Regiment. (The unit takes pride in its history of four state forces and has the likes of Maharana Pratap and now Maj Shaitan Singh, PVC as its ideals).

The remaining volunteers were sent to the Bikaner Sadul Light Infantry (now 19 Rajput). Officers were also transferred around and assigned to different regiments and units.

Shaitan Singh was assigned to the Jodhpur Sardar Infantry. Lt Col Jaswant Singh was posted to the Bikaner Sadul Light Infantry before being transferred and became the first CO of the Mewar Infantry, which was affiliated with the Rajputana Rifles, in June 1951. Maj Sangram, Maj Bhairon Singh and Maj Veer Singh were transferred to the Jat regiment, Maj Gulab Singh was transferred to 13 Kumaon while Capt Pratap Singh was sent to the Assam Regiment. Maj Shivji Singh joined the Mewar Infantry and was appointed as its second adjutant.

For about one and a half years, Shaitan Singh served as the unit's IO. He excelled in patrolling operations and also obtained expertise working in high altitudes and in harsh weather conditions.

From Kotah To Jodhpur

Soon after the merger of the Kotah Umed Infantry after its last posting at Bikaner, the officers were sent to various units. Shaitan was sent to Jodhpur Sardar Infantry on April 15th in Jasai, Barmer.

Jodhpur Sardar Infantry was an infantry battalion of the Jodhpur State Forces. I would like to briefly discuss the history of the Jodhpur Sardar Infantry with the readers to offer them more information about the unit.

The Jodhpur State was given permission to raise an infantry unit consisting of a mixed headquarters and two companies, one Rajput and one Jat, under the terms of the 1920 Indian State Forces Scheme. The Rajputs and Jats made up the infantry unit when it was raised in October 1922 under the name Sardar Infantry. The initial commander of the unit was Maj Aman Singh Bahadur, IOM. The unit was expanded to a full battalion in 1924–1925 with a mixed headquarters and four companies two Rajput and two Jat. This was completed in March 1926.

It was moved to Nowshera in November 1940 and then to Quetta. It left for foreign waters on June 10, 1941, and disembarked in Massawa, Eritrea, on June 22, 1941. It next relocated to Asmara, where it stayed for almost four months before returning to Massawa, where it was chosen to carry out guard duties for prisoners of war.

The unit was sent to Egypt in April 1942 and spent the following 13 months guarding both German and Italian POWs as well as Base Ordnance and Supply depots, where its actions significantly decreased the incidences of theft.

The battalion unexpectedly found itself designated for duty and sent to Syria in May 1943. After undergoing extensive training, it moved to Algeria for additional training before setting sail for Italy, where it landed in Salerno Bay on September 8–9, just as Italy surrendered. German soldiers continued to oppose the landing even though the unit had no losses. Following the landing, they received one DSO, Major Kunwar Ram Singh, one Military, Major Dungar Singh, one MBE, Jemadar Ganga Ram and additionally three Military Medals, and 17 Mentions in Dispatches.

Later the battalion was deployed to eastern Italy, followed by a return to Sicily. After extensive training, the battalion finally returned to its infantry role on December 10 and joined the 10th Indian Infantry Brigade, 10th Indian Division on the frontlines in Italy. Except for a brief period in April 1945 when it was under the command of 25th Indian Infantry Brigade, it remained with this formation for the remainder of the Italian campaign. During its service with the Division, the battalion saw a great deal of combat and developed a solid reputation among its contemporaries. It finally set sail for Egypt in May 1945, and later arrived in Jodhpur in August.

The battalion was chosen to join the 150th Infantry Brigade following a period of leave, and in October 1945, it left for Hong Kong. Till May 1947, when it returned to the state, it stayed there.

On April 12, 1951, the Maharana Bhupal Singh of Udaipur, as Raj Pramukh of United Rajasthan, made an appeal to the then prime minister, Jawaharlal Nehru, and minister of state, N. Gopalaswami Ayyangar, that if a unit bearing the name of Mewar could be kept in the Indian Army of the future. He also mentioned that the Maharaja of Jodhpur conveyed his heartfelt anxiety over the disbandment of all the units of Jodhpur Forces.

He wrote: "To have no regular unit bearing the name of Mewar or Jodhpur or any connection with the state seems to me almost a sacrilege."

Nehru sent the same original letter of Maharana Bhupal Singh to the defence minister stating the appeal to have units named after Jodhpur and Mewar.

The-then defence minister, Baldev Singh, in reply wrote to the Prime Minister: "We have already decided to retain the Mewar Infantry about which the maharana was very anxious. We have also decided to retain the Jodhpur Sardar Infantry. The result of this is that Jaipur, Jodhpur, Udaipur, and Bikaner will each have one infantry unit in the integrated army. Regarding Jodhpur, as I have already mentioned, we are retaining the Jodhpur Infantry."

Thus, Jodhpur Sardar Infantry was retained and continued to be a part of the Indian Army. During this time the unit under the command of Lt Col Dhonkal Singh was posted in Jasai, Barmer, which was a small military station near the border of newly formed Pakistan. The unit's main duty was to conduct border patrols to prevent any kind of cross-border crimes or trespassing. In this unit, Shaitan had friends from his schooldays, including 2/Lt Mal Singh, 2/Lt Bijai Singh, and 2/Lt Hari Singh.

Almost all the officers and troops of the unit belonged from Jodhpur State. Shaitan knew many of the people in JSI. Though he never bothered anyone for anything and always managed on his own.

On May 5, 1951, Lt Col Hem Singh died of illness that followed a paralytic attack in April. Despite treatment, he never recovered. Shaitan was told of this tragic event and he travelled to Banasar to attend his father's funeral.

While in Jodhpur Sardar Infantry, 2/Lt Shaitan Singh SF-GR 321/SS 15476 got his short service regular commission into the Indian Army with number SS-16229. If he had not got the short service regular commission, he would have been released from the service according to the state forces reorganisation scheme with some perks and grant of land. However, since he received the commission, his service was extended for five additional years.

He remained as a company officer in the JSI before being transferred to 6 Kumaon in September 1951. His friends Bijai Singh and Hari Singh were sent to 22 Pubjab and 4/9 Gorkha Rifles respectively.

In June 1954 the battalion was amalgamated into the Indian Army as 20th Battalion (Jodhpur), The Rajput Regiment, later became the 24th (Jodhpur) Battalion, Mechanised Infantry Regiment.

References

1. Interview with Mr Narpat Singh s/o Maj Shaitan Singh
2. Interview with Colonel Shivji Singh (retd)
3. Interview with Colonel Bajrang Singh (retd)
4. Documents of Lt Col Jaswant Sinh, MBE (retd)
5. Telephonic Interview with Mr Mayurdwajh Sinh Grandnephew of Lt Col Jaswant Sinh, MBE
6. Interview with Mr Haigreev Singh grandson of Col Mohan Singh
7. Interview with Mrs Sagar Kanwar d/o Col Rewat Singh, 20 Rajput
8. Telephonic conversation with Mr Digvijay Singh s/o Lt Col Durjan Sal Singh
9. Telephonic conversation with Captain Siddarth Singh (retd) grandson of Lt Col Durjan Sal Singh
10. Interview with Lt Col Daulat Singh (retd)
11. Interview with Mr Rajat Singh
12. Interview with Mr Sajjan Singh s/o AVM Chandan Singh, MVC, AVSM, VrC
13. Telephonic conversation with Maj Gen Kishan Singh (retd) s/o Brig Hari Singh, AVSM
14. OTS joining letter of Major Shaitan Singh
15. Documents of Major Shaitan Singh
16. Book: *The Maharajas Paltans : A History of the Indian State Forces 1888-1948* by Richard Head and Tony McClenaghan

❑

Bedu Pako Baramasa

Days in Six Kumaon

Lt Shaitan Singh, 6 Kumaon

This chapter on Maj Shaitan Singh's tenure with 6 Kumaon in Shillong and Trivandrum focuses on the special role and intensive training done by the battalion and some life events of Major Shaitan Singh during 1951-53.

West to East

The date was September 6, 1951. It was a pleasant Thursday in Shillong, which is now the capital of Meghalaya. A young officer alighted from a state transport vehicle after a very long journey. He had come all the way from Jasai, a small garrison located in Rajasthan's Barmer.

The young officer was sent on a new posting, a permanent transfer. It was his first posting with any regular battalion of the Indian Army. Before that he had served with three Indian state forces units.

There were various issues on his mind. For the first time he was going to serve with officers from all India. While he was in the Jodhpur Sardar Infantry, he had a certain comfort level as he served with his friends whom he knew from his school days. But here, everyone and everything was new to him.

A vehicle was there to pick him up and take him to the Elephant Falls, where the unit was located. The unit that he had joined was the 6 Kumaon or now popularly known as the Jangi Six. 6 Kumaon is a former Hyderabad regiment unit. (The battalion served in the Second World War, Operation Polo in 1948, the 1962 India-China War, the 1965 India- Pakistan War and the 1971 Bangladesh Liberation War.)

The security of India's eastern borders became a concern for the government soon after Independence. For millennia, tribal communities had resided in the jungle-covered, roadless mountains near the India-Burma border. They had led independent lives devoid of any onerous government restrictions. Although the area was ideal for infiltration by insurgent groups, the Indian government did not want to meddle with tribal affairs. The area had to be effectively patrolled to avoid this risk. It was the 6th Kumaon battalion that was assigned with this experimental task.

After the police operations in Hyderabad, where the unit had confronted the Razakars — a Muslim militia formed by Majlis-e-Ittehadul Muslimeen leader Bahadur Yar Jung to resist Hyderabad's merger with India — and brought an end to the turmoil in the Warangal district, the battalion arrived in Shillong towards the end of 1948 at the Elephant Falls, which is in Upper Shillong near Y-Junction Shillong-Dawki and Shillong-Mawphlang. Since there were so few troops in the erstwhile undivided Assam and just one brigade guarding the area of Nagaland, Mizoram, and Nefa (North-East Frontier Agency), the battalion was used for both routine tasks and its special role.

The unit was a part of the 181 Infantry Brigade Group which was then commanded by Brig (later Lt Gen) Bikram Singh. Bikram Singh was a man of action and judgement; he dealt with inefficiency in a strong and brutal manner, and he was unwilling to compromise on efficiency. He visited the unit and always took updates of the affairs of the battalion.

Lt Col Kaman Singh, MVC of the Garhwal Rifles, was hand-selected in August 1950 to lead the 6 Kumaon for its unique duty. Kaman Singh was a skilled officer with a prestigious reputation. He led the 3rd Battalion, Garhwal Rifles, before moving to 6 Kumaon. The 3 Garhwal participated in the 1947–1948 Operations with distinction under the command of Lt Col Kaman Singh. They were awarded the Battle Honour "Tithwal" and became one of the most decorated battalions in the Indian Army.

In one operation, they received 1 MVC, 18 VrCs, 1 Ashoka Chakra Class III, and 19 Mentions in Dispatches. Kaman Singh was an ideal candidate to lead a battalion in a special role because he had demonstrated his mettle and courage during the 1948 India-Pakistan War.

Dine-In: A New Beginning

When the young officer finally reached the unit's location, he reported to the adjutant, Capt Bakhtawar Singh Brar. Capt Brar briefed him about the Battalion. A soldier escorted the subaltern to his room in the officers' accommodation. In the evening the subaltern received an invitation to the officers' mess for the "dining-in" ceremony, where all the officers of the units were present with the ladies. Capt Bakhtawar introduced him to other officers. "Let us all welcome 2/Lt Shaitan Singh to the Six Kumaon."

The officers of 6 Kumaon planned the dinner, and a band played music in the background. Following the dinner, everyone congregated in the mess's anteroom where speeches were delivered, and toasts were proposed. The freshly inducted Shaitan was offered a drink, but he declined saying, "Gentlemen, I'm sorry, but I don't drink; I'm a teetotaller." Lt Jaswant Singh playfully remarked, "Tum Shaitan ho nahi (you don't seem Shaitan)," to which everyone chuckled.

Shaitan had one peculiarity: everyone considered him to be the opposite of what his name suggested. His demeanour was always one of peace and gentleness.

The subaltern was personally greeted by the commandant, who inquired about his prior military service and family. When the commandant learned about Shaitan's father, who had a stellar record of service, he was impressed. He gave Shaitan one piece of advice: "Shaitan, always believe in your abilities, you will make a big name someday." Then he wished him well.

Then, Shaitan was taken to sign the visitors' book while the other officers casually discussed things. The company commander, Major P.H. Honawar, placed a hand on Shaitan's shoulder and gently apprised him to be prefared for the impending busy schedule and demanding training that they had been undergoing for a few years now.

Shaitan responded saying, "I am fully prepared for the upcoming task, Sir. My career began with a harsh field posting. I've seen worse; there were times when I had to spend nights in sub-zero temperatures, climbing the mountains of Drass while on patrol. So, it will not be a problem for me. I am physically and mentally ready for it."

Due to a government mandate that state forces officers had to forfeit five years of seniority if they had chosen to serve in the Indian Army, Shaitan Singh was still a second lieutenant even after nearly five years of service. It was a perception that since the former states lacked adequate training facilities, the state forces officers too would not be trained suitably. Hence, these officers had to forfeit their significant ranks and five years of seniority.

The next day, September 7, 2/Lt Shaitan Singh joined the unit officially. He was assigned to the Alpha company which was an Ahir company. As the 6th Battalion the Kumaon Regiment was composed of 75 per cent Kumaoni troops and 25 per cent Ahir troops. The Ahir troops constituted the Alpha company.

The role of the battalion was to carry out training to gain expertise in weapons and equipment with suitability for long-range penetration patrols along the lines of the famous Chindits Brigade during the Burma campaign where the British Brig Orde Wingate formed the Chindits for raiding operations against the Imperial Japanese Army, especially undertaking long-range penetrations and attacking Japanese troops, facilities, and their lines of communication deep behind Japanese lines.

(The Chindits operations featured long marches through extremely difficult terrain, often undertaken by underfed malnourished troops weakened by diseases, like malaria and dysentery. Controversy persists over the extremely high casualty-rate and the debatable military value of the achievements of the Chindits.)

Re-Organisation of 6 Kumaon

The battalion was reorganised on the lines of paratrooper rifles. It had battalion headquarters, three rifle companies, each made up of four platoons, with a support company and an administration company. The companies were commanded by majors and support platoons were commanded by subalterns. The unit always had 6 majors, including the second in command. The transport platoon was the backbone of the unit during the patrols, it had six horses and 120 mules to provide support to the troops during training and patrols. Also, during the whole tenure officers from the Remount Veterinary Corps with staff were attached to the unit to look after its animals.

Troops were equipped with lighter weight .303 rifles and officers with STENs (or Sten guns) with a pistol as a personal weapon.

Shaitan joined the unit and became familiar with the organisation and regular procedures of the unit. On September 23, he received a letter stating that he had been selected to attend the 3-inch mortar course at the Weapons Wing Infantry School, Mhow, starting from October 1, 1951.

Shaitan had just spent 20 days in the unit when he was chosen to attend the course. Therefore, the next day, the commandant of the unit called him to his office. The CO asked him if he wanted to attend the course or not. He told Shaitan that if he didn't want to opt for this course he could ask the officials to arrange for him to attend the next course. Shaitan gave it a thought and told his CO that he didn't want to miss the opportunity and would like to attend the course. The CO readily agreed and said, "Do your best son, make us proud, get ready and pack your luggage."

Shaitan left the office happily and came to his accommodation to pack his luggage.

3” Mortar Course

The next day, September 25, Shaitan left for Mhow. In those days, it generally took three to four days of travelling to reach Mhow from Shillong. First, one had to travel by state transport to Guwahati and from there a long train journey of three days to Mhow.

On September 29, Shaitan reported to the Infantry School. There he got his accommodation. It was his second course at Mhow so he was familiar with the environment and the rules of the place. Soon, on October 1, the two months-long course commenced under the supervision of Major Rai Singh, who was the senior instructor of the course. The course mainly focused on the theoretical fundamentals, where the students were taught about the design, working and usages of the battalion weapon – 3-inch mortar, followed by weekly tests before the practical tests. It meant firing practices of the weapon at the mortar-firing range in Mhow. During the course, 2/Lt Shaitan Singh was promoted to the rank of lieutenant.

The course ended on December 1 with a group photograph of instructors and students. Shaitan did well in the course and got a good grade.

After the course ended, he applied for his annual leave, which he was granted. This time he got a 40-day leave.

Shaitan reached home on December 8 after two days of travel. This was the first time he went home after his father’s death. Things had changed considerably by then. He had new responsibilities and was now the head of the household. This time, his leave was spent running to government offices to get documents organised after his father’s death. He was able to spend time during the end of his leave to visit Jodhpur to meet his relatives and brothers, Lal Singh and Prithvi Singh, and also his son, Narpat, who were studying in Chopasni School.

On January 16, 1952, Shaitan left for Shillong and it took him three days to reach the battalion location near Garampani. He rejoined the unit on January 19 and got back to regular duties. On January 26, 1952, India's third Republic Day, Lt Shaitan was appointed officiating adjutant of 6 Kumaon. Shaitan did his adjutant's duties for some time and he was again sent to the field as his battalion was preparing for a long-range patrol.

Though Shaitan did not participate in all the patrols and activities, I would like to share the basic details of tough training and operations conducted by 6 Kumaon.

Training

The battalion, after its reorganisation and receiving the equipment and weapons, carried out intensive training in jungles and hilly areas of Assam during 1949-50. The focus was on rigorous physical and mental training, because, for a guerrilla, it was critical to be physically and mentally fit. The priority was always given to toughen up the men and maximum emphasis was on route marches with full battle load and rucksack 08, a big backpack in which soldiers carry their belongings according to operations. The daily routine of the battalion included route marches with complete FSMO (field-scale march-out order) with full load. Intensive physical training, long walks and runs, and cross-country runs were the normal exercises.

Collective training included self-contained company columns on long-range patrols of several days. These involved complete administrative support for men and animals on man/mule pack basis, movement through jungle and hilly terrain, crossing of streams and rivers with improvised methods, laying ambushes on given points, raids on pre-selected or opportunity targets, demolition of vital points in the enemy rear and retrieving air-dropped supplies.

Route marches from Shillong to Jowal Farm, which was nearly 30 miles, with loads were normal. Everyone in the battalion had to cover this distance in 16 hours before they could qualify for annual leave. With constant practice, it became very easy for everyone, including the Non Combatant Support Elements or NCSEs.

Long-range penetration patrols in the form of self-contained company columns with animal transport and detachments of battalion weapons were regularly conducted deep in the jungles. The duration of these patrols would be any time between one and three weeks. The emphasis of these patrols was individual physical fitness, maximum use of local resources and developing high standards of junior leadership. The subalterns of the unit, including Shaitan Singh, Lakha Singh, Surajnath Nagar, and TV Rama Rao, were always used to lead the recce (reconnaissance) platoon before the long-range patrol.

During the winter months, the battalion moved out to a place called Garampani for intensive jungle training under the new role and to carry out river-crossing exercises. The unit organised a demonstration on "assault river crossing" with only improvised water manoeuvres for the benefit of all troops in 181 Independent Brigade Group. It proved a great success.

This earnest and sincere work enhanced the prestige and efficiency of the unit in the eyes of one and all in the brigade group, and the brigade commander congratulated the unit for the best work. During this period, when the battalion was in Garampani, long-range patrols with durations of four days, seven days, and 10 days were sent out to try out the suitability of the equipment and organisation of the battalion. The battalion had trained so well that the longest organised patrol could cover 200 miles in 10 days without a single OR (other rank/below officer rank) falling out.

General Intelligence Course for Officers

Soon, by the end of March 1952, Shaitan was called for the general intelligence course at the Intelligence Training School and Depot, Mhow, starting on April 1. The school was located at Karachi before Independence and later it moved to Ambala just after Partition in 1947.

In November 1947, the school moved to Mhow where the first post-Independence course commenced in October 1948. Shaitan joined the school two days prior to the course. The 40-day-long course started on April 1 under the command of Maj C.S. Hiran.

In those 40 days, the role of the Intelligence Training School and Depot was to impart training in intelligence and security to officers through conducting regular theory classes and tests.

In this course Shaitan had a coursemate named Lt A.O. Alexander, who later went on to command 16 Madras and raised 27 Madras just a few months before the 1971 operations. He was killed in action in the Kutch sector, while participating in the war with his unit.

The course ended on May 10, 1952, and just after the completion of the course Shaitan was immediately recalled to rejoin the battalion. In four days Shaitan rejoined the unit.

Operations and LRPs

The battalion was tasked to send out long-range patrols. Initially, they sent long patrols for about 50–80 miles but soon the range of patrol was increased to check out the suitability of training and equipment.

Company columns with more than 100 mules were sent out from Shillong. Out of a number of columns, the following two may be specially mentioned as they were the most difficult:

It was late in the year 1951, one company column covered approximately 200 miles. From Shillong to Halflong and beyond, through the jungle tracks.

In 1952, one operational patrol was planned, in which a company column ran from Shillong to Kohima (Nagaland) also through jungle tracks covering nearly 300 miles. Replenishment of supplies was arranged by air dropping through the-then HQ Eastern Command, Ranchi. This operation was carried out successfully, with zero casualties.

The column involved in this patrol covered the longest distance. It was with this column that saw the graveyard of the casualties of the Second World War. Thousands of soldiers resting in peace on a ridge near the town in the heart of Nagaland jungles and the engraving on the memorial pillar: "When you go home, tell them of us and say, for their tomorrow we gave our today."

This sight created a feeling of sober serenity which extended an invitation for all the soldiers to come again and pay their homage to the brave. Sure enough, the Indian Army had to operate again on a large scale in Nagaland in the years to come.

Both columns moved on a man/mule pack basis with seven days' provisions on man and the balance on mules. The columns were self-contained in arms and equipment, but rations and ammunition were replenished en route through air drops in pre-arranged drop zones in the jungles. The movements were mostly during the day for obvious reasons and the columns harboured at night.

One platoon under a subaltern moved about half an hour in advance to recce and mark the routes through jungle, prepare diversions for animals where necessary, select crossing places in case of river/streams and recce a site for the harbour area in the evening. It saved a lot of time for the main column and ensured speed in movement.

The columns moved through a part of Nagaland and one of the aims was to make the presence of the Indian Army visible and check on the attitude of the local population. Various patrols in different parts discovered that unrest was brewing, and their main complaint was that the civil administration never bothered to go into the interior areas and look after them. This kind of information was always included in the long-range patrol reports, which were submitted at the end of the operations. The battalion always tried to maintain a peaceful relationship with the locals.

Once, two companies of the battalion were employed in a special role to operate against the strongholds of communist insurgents in several villages. They earned the goodwill of the local population by ensuring that the local territory was free of insurgents.

During all these operations and training, Shaitan Singh participated in patrols and other activities of the unit. It was July when Shillong was under heavy monsoon rains. The battalion was still conducting training in dampened forests and hills. Shaitan received a letter from home apprising him of a few functions and ceremonies, including the wedding of his brother Surajbhan Singh, which he and his family had fixed during his last leave. He applied for the leave but as mentioned earlier, everyone in the battalion had to participate in a route march from Shillong to Jowal Farm and cover nearly 30 miles with pack on, in 16 hours before one could qualify for annual leave.

Shaitan also participated in one such route march and easily completed it. After all, the 6 Kumaon had regularly trained for such marches. Shaitan got an annual leave of 48 days from July 14. Again, it took four days of an exhausting journey to reach home.

This time at home, he had to look after arranging his younger brother's wedding. In those days there were no shopping facilities in his village or nearby. For all the shopping related to the wedding, he went to Jodhpur where he met Lt Mal Singh of Jodhpur Sardar Infantry, his dear friend or rather, should I say, his brother from another mother. Shaitan had already discussed the wedding related shopping with Mal Singh.

Both went to a cycle shop to rent two cycles for a day to go to various places and markets. When they reached the shop and asked the owner to provide them two cycles, on rent, the shop owner readily agreed and asked both to submit the advance payment and some kind of identity document. When Shaitan submitted his ID card, the shop owner looked at it and read the name "Shaitan". Curious, he asked, "What is your name?" Shaitan replied, "My name is Shaitan Singh." The person gave him a strange look and laughed saying, "You don't look Shaitan."

When Shaitan received such a look and was laughed at for his name, he disliked his name even more.

Both Shaitan and Mal Singh completed their shopping and returned in the evening. When they had to go to the cycle shop to return the cycles, Shaitan didn't go into the shop. He stood outside the shop as he knew the owner would again make fun of his name. When Mal Singh came out of the shop, he asked Shaitan why he had not come inside. Shaitan replied, "I did not like the way he joked about my name in the morning. If I had come inside, he would certainly have joked about my name again."

He told Mal Singh that he didn't like his name as everyone made fun of it, sometimes in the unit, even on the courses too. He asked Mal Singh, "What should I do now?" Mal Singh suggested that Shaitan could try to apply to change his name.

This suggestion was now engraved in Shaitan's mind.

He went back home and again got engaged in wedding arrangements. A few days later the ceremonies started and Surajbhan Singh got married. After the wedding Shaitan received a letter from the unit. It said after his leave was over, he should go to Namkum, Ranchi for an anti-malaria hygiene course.

Anti Malaria Hygiene Course

Soon after the leave ended, Shaitan went to Namkum for a 20-day-long anti-malaria hygiene course. In those days, malaria was an epidemic. The entire country, be it villages or cities, was affected by it and killed thousands of people. In the early 1950s, every year in India, around 7.5 crore people contracted malaria and approximately 800,000 died from the disease. So, the Indian Army came up with a course of personal and surrounding hygiene for its officers and troops to prevent the troops from getting the disease. As Shaitan's unit was located and operating in jungle areas in the northeast; it was more important for them to be cautious and stay healthy.

In this course, Shaitan learned about the disease, the causes of its spread and the treatment for malaria. They were asked to stay in nets and use anti-mosquito lotions. Also, the most important lesson of this course was to make one learn how to maintain hygiene and prevent malaria, and also stay safe from the parasitic mosquito.

Shaitan did so well in this course that he got the best gradings.

After the completion of the course, he returned to join his unit. The day he reached the unit he asked the cook of the mess to make some sweets. The cook surprisingly asked: "Sahab, what happened? Is there any special occasion?" To which Shaitan replied: "It was my brother's wedding last month. I could have bought sweets from Jodhpur where they make some delicious sweets but I had to go for a course to Ranchi so I could not bring them myself. Can you make some for dinner tonight?"

In the evening, all the officers enjoyed the meal, especially the sweets. Everyone praised and congratulated Shaitan.

I Want to Change My Name

On October 1, Shaitan went to meet the CO at his office. The CO asked Shaitan, "What happened son?"

Shaitan, in a gentle tone replied, "Sir, I want to change my name."

The CO, a bit surprised, asked, "Did I hear it right that you want to change your name?"

Shaitan: "Yes, Sir, I want to change my name."

The CO: "But why?"

Shaitan: "Sir, firstly, I don't like my name and ..."

The CO: "And what?"

Shaitan: "Sir, everyone makes fun of my name - sometimes in the unit and even on courses people make fun of me. They also give me the code name 'Shaitan'."

The CO: "Son, I know you, you are totally the opposite of your name. You are a very kind and a sincere person. Let them tease you, it should not affect you."

Shaitan: "Sir, since my school days, I've been tolerating this. People give me add looks after listening to my name. Even my real name is Udaibhan Singh."

The CO: "If your real name is Udaibhan Singh then how come you are called Shaitan Singh?"

Shaitan: "Sir, my father's British senior sometimes called me Shaitan in my childhood and my father registered this name in school without giving a thought."

The CO: "All right, I understand what you feel. I assure you that I will see what can be done in this matter."

Shaitan: "Thank you, Sir, I really want to change this name now."

Several days later, the commanding officer asked Shaitan to meet him in his office. Shaitan went to the office where the CO handed him an application form to apply for a name change. Shaitan happily looked at the CO and thanked him.

Shaitan filled up the form and submitted it to the CO. The CO processed the form and sent it to the 181 Brigade Group. However, the application got rejected. A week later, Shaitan got to know about it. He again asked the CO for the application. They applied for it again and the result was the same - rejected.

On November 9, 1952, Shaitan sent an application, one last time, to change his name from Shaitan Singh to Udaibhan Singh giving a reason that the correct name according to horoscopes is Udaibhan Singh and Shaitan Singh was just a pet name in childhood days that was wrongly registered in the school. He added that the name did not sound appropriate, and he felt like changing it. The CO on November 12 processed it and sent it to the brigade headquarters.

On November 14, the brigade rejected the application with a note that read: "The application for the change of name in respect to Lt Shaitan Singh is returned herewith for resubmission together with documentary evidence to show that the correct name of the officer is Udaibhan Singh."

This time when the CO got to know the reason for the rejection of Shaitan's application for changing his name, he asked Shaitan to meet him. Shaitan met him and had a conversation.

CO: "The application got rejected this time too. But they can reconsider your application if you can produce any documentary evidence to prove that your name is Udaibhan Singh."

Shaitan: "Sir, I don't have any document supporting the claim as my name in all my documents is Shaitan Singh, even in all my marksheets."

CO: "Son, now I feel this name is always going to be with you. You will be known by this name. Never get affected by what others say about it."

Shaitan sadly left the office knowing nothing could be done now. He would always be known as Shaitan to which he was the exact opposite.

(Little did he know at that time that this name — Shaitan — would be engraved in the golden words of time one day.)

Double-Day and a General's Visit

Lt Col Shankar Lal Sharma, who completed the whole tenure in Shillong with the unit from 1949 to 1953 wrote: "Once a week, a 'double day' was observed when everyone moved from one point to another within the unit lines with troops bearing dual responsibilities in their employment (which meant carrying out their regular duties with more than regular speed). The movement would also include the unit's commanding officer and subedar major.

A very interesting anecdote about double day includes the-then Eastern Army commander, Lt Gen Nathu Singh. He happened to drop in at the battalion on a double day. While driving through the lines, he observed that several personnel, including officers and JCOs, were running here and there. He got curious and stopped his car to ask a passing soldier about what had happened in the lines. The soldier halted and gave a crisp salute to the general and replied, "Nothing, Sa'ab," and started running again. After a few yards away, he found the Sub Maj Arjun Singh doubling the quarter guard with the treasure chest book. At last, the perplexed general asked the CO what the matter was. The VIP got a negative reply from the CO as he said, "Nothing happened, Sir," to which the general asked, "But I saw a number of your chaps, including officers and the subedar major, running from place to place today."

The CO chuckled after he understood the general's curiosity and explained, "Sir, it was a double day in the battalion as a part of our toughening-up training." Hearing this, the VIP laughed as he was concerned that there had been an emergency in the unit.

A month passed in regular activities of the unit. The new year, 1953, started and the battalion received orders to convert back to a regular infantry battalion. The re-organisation started, and it took some time to return to normalcy after three long years of rigorous physical and mental training coupled with similar operations. Although patrolling continued, they were no longer hundred-mile-long ones as before.

In February, the battalion received orders to move to Trivandrum (now Thiruvananthapuram), the capital of Kerala. The advance party of the unit moved to Trivandrum to make arrangements for the unit. In March, the whole battalion started packing and handing over responsibilities.

Besides military training and operations, the unit also excelled in sports and social activities. Once the unit defeated all other local units to win the Fraternity Cup of the Shillong subarea. The unit under Lt Col Kaman Singh performed well throughout the tenure and outperformed all sister units in training and battle exercises.

Move to Trivandrum

Maj Manjeet Brar, son of Maj Bakhtawar Singh Brar, a 109-year-old Kumaoni, was just five at that time. He remembers that around March 20, the unit moved by road to the nearest railway station at Guwahati, which was almost 100 kilometres away from Shillong. From there they had to board a special military train. The unit boarded the train and loaded the luggage in covered wagons.

The Pandu-Amingaon train ferry across the mile-wide Brahmaputra river was a bottleneck in the metre-gauge rail system. The ferry loading point was hazardous. Here, the mighty river was also very deep. The train's wagons had to be disjointed, remarshalled, and loaded on the ferry. It was already evening and the bricks put by the ferry staff to mark the end point fell into the water and some wagons were moved much behind the mark. As a result, they fell into the Brahmaputra, never to be found again. Those wagons took away some records, luggage, and some silver of the battalion as well.

Attempts were made to get to the wagons with the help of divers, but failed and the unit was ordered to move ahead.

On March 31, the unit reached Trivandrum. The city is on India's southwest and is bounded by the Laccadive Sea to its west and the Western Ghats to its east. The unit was located at Pangode military station, which was the headquarters of the Nair Brigade or the Travancore Army till 1954. Shaitan had little knowledge about the Travancore State Forces. During his General Intelligence Course he had a coursemate called A.O. Alexander, a lieutenant from the Punjab Regiment. However, Lt Alexander was a former Travancore State Forces officer. He had told Shaitan about the state forces because both belonged to different state forces. Shaitan's unit was now under the Southern Army Command, the oldest field formation of the Indian Army. At that time, the Southern Command was commanded by Lt Gen

SM Srinagesh, who was Shaitan's unit's former commanding officer from December 17, 1942 to August 28, 1945. Shrinagesh was the CO of the 6/19 Hyderabad Regiment, which had now become the 6 Kumaon.

The Kumaoni troops were uncomfortable with the weather and it took them some time to settle down. On the very first day in Trivandrum, Lt Shaitan Singh was given a new responsibility. He was appointed the 3-inch mortar platoon commander of 6 Kumaon as he was the only one among junior officers to have done the 3-inch mortar course.

In May, Lt Col Harbans Singh Virk, MVC, DSO came to the unit as he was to take over the command from Lt Col Kaman Singh, MVC. Lt Col Kaman was chosen to lead 6 Assam Rifles in Agartala as he had already commanded 6 Kumaon in the area. Kaman Singh relinquished command of the unit on May 29, 1953. A farewell party was organised for this legendary officer. He left the unit on May 3. (Lt Col Kaman. Singh took over the command of 6 Assam Rifles in Agartala on 4 June 1953, where he continued to participate in anti-militancy operations. At a young age of 39, he had already commanded three different units, and on July 3, 1956, he was chosen to take over the command of 3 Kumaon (Rifles) and was posted in Uri Sector in Jammu & Kashmir. On July 15, 1956, during a visit to a high-altitude post, soon after having tea on his way up, he collapsed and died. He was 39.)

On May 30, Lt Col H.S. Virk, a Second World War and First India-Pakistan War veteran, who led the 3 Para Maratha Light Infantry with great success against the Pakistani forces at Naushera. His tactical skills not only led to several successful attacks on the enemy but also saved the Indian garrison at Naushera during the famous battle of "Kala Gosh Galla". His most notable achievement, however, was the recapture of Jhangar, where the lieutenant colonel was honoured with the Mahavir Chakra in recognition of his outstanding leadership; he now took over the command of 6 Kumaon. Being a war veteran, he was a hard taskmaster who focused on the training and physical fitness of his men.

Soon on June 1, Shaitan was promoted to the rank of acting captain and was appointed as company commander of his unit's Bravo Company, because various officers of the unit were either transferred or sent on courses. He now had two responsibilities: one being the mortar platoon commander and another new and important one as company commander.

Subedar and Hony Capt Man Singh, who himself is a 1962 India-China war veteran, who fought in the Battle of Walong along with the Delta Company of 6 Kumaon under Lt Bikram Singh, was a young recruit in 1953. He reminisces that Trivandrum was a peace posting and the unit was independent as the brigade was at a distance. He recalls Shaitan Singh as a very simple gentleman, a competent officer who had a good command of his men and took care of them like his family. He spent almost five months with Shaitan Singh in 6 Kumaon. He added that wherever Shaitan Singh took over the command, he did well. He went to 13 Kumaon, where he and his company fought braverly and suffered heavy casualties but foiled the attempts of the Chinese in Ladakh.

Dining Out

In October, Shaitan received his transfer order. He was now being sent to the Kumaon Regimental Centre at Ranikhet, which was then in Uttar Pradesh and now in Uttarakhand. On October 9, a "Dining Out" party was organised for him. There were many new faces in the battalion. Some of those who had dined-in Shaitan, like the former CO Lt Col Kaman Singh, had already left the unit. He had profound emotions about this. He had joined the unit as a young subaltern, where he had lived for two years, made a few close friends, and formed relationships that would last a lifetime. He was now leaving his parent unit as an accomplished captain. Any officer who moved to a new unit or posting found it emotionally challenging to leave his parent unit.

On October 10, 1953, Captain Shaitan Singh moved to Ranikhet, without knowing that he would never come to his parent unit 6 Kumaon again.

Since its formation during the Second World War, when it was involved in the war against the Japanese, 6 Kumaon has continuously been in action. Following independence, the battalion took part in several operations. Although sustaining significant losses in the 1962 conflict with the Chinese, the unit heroically battled in the NEFA's Walong area and was the only one to counterattack the Chinese position. The unit fought in Ichhogil Canal in the 1965 conflict with Pakistan. In the Shakargarh sector of the 1971 Bangladesh Liberation War, the unit once more demonstrated its mettle. In addition, the unit has received numerous honours and distinctions in both times of war and peace, carrying on the tradition of its forebears. They feel proud calling themselves Jangi.

References

1. Telephonic Interview with Lt Col N.S. Pathania (retd) s/o Lt Col Kaman Singh
2. Telephonic Interview with Mr Kamaljeet Singh Pathania s/o Lt Col Kaman Singh
3. Telephonic Interview with Major Manjeet Brar (retd) s/o Maj B.S. Brar
4. Interview with Honorary Captain Man Singh, 6 Kumaon (retd)
5. Telephonic conversation with Col Akhil Sharma (retd) s/o Lt Col S.L. Sharma
6. Book *Valour Triumphs: A History of the Kumaon Regiment* Hardcover by K.C. Praval

❑

The Captain

At the Home of Kumaon

Captain Shaitan Singh, Kumaon Regimental Centre

This chapter focuses on the tenure of Major Shaitan Singh at Ranikhet when he was a young captain. At the centre, he was given an opportunity to lead a training company, which was aimed to train new recruits and turn them into fine soldiers for the various battalions of the regiment. In later years at the centre, he was given a very demanding task – the duty of quartermaster. His tenure at the centre was the longest posting with any institution or battalion that lasted four years.

A History of Home of Kumaon

The Kumaon Hills, the homeland of the Kumaonis, are situated in the shadow of the snow-capped Himalayas, halfway between Nepal and India's Garhwal district. The home of the Kumaon Regiment, Ranikhet, is surrounded by beautiful hills and resort towns. The scenic place earned it the popular name "Queen of the Highlands".

The Kumaon Regimental Centre's relocation from Agra to Ranikhet in May 1948, when the British left the barracks, was the primary significant event. For individuals in a regiment, a regimental centre serves as an equivalent of home. When the time comes to lay down their arms, they return there where they began their careers. And when they return to their native places, they turn to the regimental centre for assistance. It makes sense that it would work better if it were adjacent to the area where the regiment recruits. Therefore, the Kumaonis, who make up most of the regiment, benefited from the Kumaon Regimental Centre's shift to Ranikhet.

The regimental centre at Ranikhet was honoured when the centre's commandant Lt Col M.R. Yadava, who was an ex-commanding officer of the 6 Kumaon who led the unit in Operation Polo to liberate Hyderabad, led team of officers, JCOs and ORs to host the-then Prime Minister Pandit Jawaharlal Nehru during his visit there, on September 26, 1953. A few days later, in the pleasant month of October 1953, a young captain was welcomed to its doors.

Ranikhet was quite far from Trivandrum. To get to the centre, one had to disembark at the Kathgodam railway station and board a vehicle to travel by road. Shaitan had to travel a very long and exhausting distance to get to the centre. The centre is stunningly beautiful. It lies in the foothills of the Himalayas and has a long and fascinating history.

The English explorer Norman Troup settled on Troup Hill - the highest point of this uninhabited land, which is now home to the administration battalion of the Kumaon Regimental Centre. This was how Ranikhet, which is located between 6,200 and 7,000 feet above sea level, got its start.

Troup became the sole owner of an immense area and planted tea plants all along the slope of these hills. A visit by Bishop Hebor to this region, in 1824, marked a turning point. The bishop was so enamoured by the beauty and tranquillity of these hills after seeing the open spaces and slopes of lush green tea plantations that he convinced the British government in Delhi to turn this area into a military cantonment and construct a retreat for English soldiers to escape the heat of the plains.

Thereafter, each one of Troup's tea plantations was purchased by the British government. A team of English engineers was subsequently dispatched, and soon a miniature version of England with lengthy military barracks with green roofs and red roofs appeared. As a result, a cantonment board was founded by 1869 and continues to oversee the management of the military cantonment today.

Troup had already lost his property by this point and relocated south to Chaubatia, where his opulent bungalow still stands as a monument. It serves as a reminder of the luxurious lifestyle of this early Ranikhet resident. The property is currently owned and operated by its current owner as the "Holm Farm Heritage Hotel" — a charming establishment that still upholds the tradition passed down through the centuries.

A lovely township was planned by the early English engineers. The entire hillside was cleared of vegetation to facilitate seamless construction of the roads and homes. Careful planning ensured that after felling the trees for the construction of roads and buildings, new trees were systematically planted afterwards. The mother plants came from England. At Chaubatia, a lovely fruit orchard and nursery was constructed, containing a variety of fruits, including apples, apricots, pears, peaches, plums, peach nuts, hazelnuts, etc. It still draws tourists to Ranikhet.

Ranikhet is already a walker's paradise, but its impressively large roads for a hill station only serve to enhance this. Beautiful bungalows line both sides of the Upper and Lower Mall Road, with names like Chester Field, Windy Ho, Belle View, Ridgeway, West View, Cleave Cottage, Priory, Rose Mount, Fir Hill, Jegati Mount and Long View. The newer additions are named Kumaon Lodge, Kumaon Mess, and Kumaon Villa. The magnificent trees, such as pine, deodar, oak, and rhododendron, that can be seen everywhere in Ranikhet is a result of this amazing planning.

These bungalows, roads, and trees are reminiscent of a bygone era.

The Ranikhet Club, a different monument that can be seen on the Upper Mall's slopes, was created in 1918. With its multiple tennis courts, beautiful green lawns, and flowerbeds brimming with the finest flowers whose seeds were brought from the renowned Valley of Flowers, which is now a national park in Uttarakhand's Chamoli district. The bungalow was a picture of architectural beauty. Foreign dignitaries and members of the British civil and military aristocracy frequented the club, which was the centre of attraction and action. Unfortunately, an unintentional fire in 1987 burned the club. It has been renovated since and, today, it is back to its former splendour. The club continues to exhibit Lt Col Noel Frederick Barwell's old photograph with pride. Now, it is a thriving institution again.

Since 1932, horses have been tethered at the Nar Singh Ground, and the ancient shed, which still stands, served as a stable. Two exquisitely built churches, St. Peter's Church and the Presbyterian Church, which both contain the "Shawl Factory" and are maintained and used for welfare activities (for war widows and retired people) by the Kumaon Regimental Centre, border the ground on either side.

Ranikhet has many churches that date back several centuries. They were constructed for all branches of Christianity. The buildings are works of art and ought to be protected as cultural treasures. The Nar Singh Ground, the sole field accessible to the residents of Ranikhet, is now the hub of all cultural events. Regardless of the event, whether it be a religious speech, a school fair, the local "Annual Autumn Festival", or Ram Lila, people from all walks of life throng to the Nar Singh Ground. Over time, this area now represents the brotherhood connection between the military and civilian population, which unites everyone in this particular township.

A Diwali with Family After Years

On October 14, 1953, Shaitan Singh became a full-time officer of the Kumaon Regimental Centre. But not long after starting at the centre, he applied for his overdue annual leave to go home. His last visit to Banasar was in September 1952. On October 22, he left for Jodhpur after having his leave approved. In those days, it was challenging to obtain a simple means of transportation for such a long and arduous journey. Officers and soldiers travelling to and from the regimental centre could count on a dependable service from Kathgodam, which served as the only railway station in the area.

Shaitan travelled home by rail on October 24 and stayed with his family for over a month. Diwali was a special occasion during this annual break. Diwali is a religious Hindu festival that is celebrated during the Hindu lunisolar months of Ashvin and Kartika (between mid-October and mid-November). This was his first Diwali with his family since enlisting in the Army, and it was also his first without his father, who died in May 1951.

Shaitan had brought gifts and presents for his family members while travelling from Jodhpur. Coming on leave during Diwali had a significant benefit for him because he could finally see all his family members together and share time during a major festival with them. The main Diwali festival was celebrated on November 6. The day began with greetings and ended with an appetising dinner, which he shared with his family and friends. Everyone assembled in their new attire in the evening to perform a Lakshmi Pujan, which was followed by the lighting of lamps and firecrackers.

The following day, Lakshmi Pujan is observed as Govardhan Puja in some rural communities in India's northern, western, and central regions. This honours the legend of the Hindu god Krishna rescuing the farming and cow-herding communities from endless rains and floods brought on by Indra's wrath by lifting the Govardhan mountain. By performing the custom of erecting tiny, miniature mountains out of cow dung and worshipping the cattle, this narrative is kept alive. An agricultural theme and celebration of the significance of cow dung to yearly crop cycles is the ritual usage of cow excrement. Govardhan Puja is one of the most important festivals in Rajasthan and is observed by virtually the entire population of the state. Additionally, Shaitan's family observed this event, and worship their cattle, and to this day they own some cows, who they worship and care for.

The remainder of the leave went by, and when the day to return to Ranikhet arrived, Shaitan and his family said their final goodbyes to one another with sadness. Shaitan boarded a train in Jodhpur and travelled via Lucknow to Kathgodam. On November 23, the day after he returned to the centre, he was given the position of training company commander of the regimental centre's training battalion.

A New Appointment

An organisation called the Infantry Training Battalion helps recruited soldiers to develop into disciplined, physically strong, and motivated infantry soldiers. The physical and mental boundaries of prospective soldiers are pushed by this fundamental training regimen. Four companies make up for one training battalion, each of which is led by a captain or a major. Captain Shaitan Singh was in charge of one such training company.

A training company commander's responsibility is to teach a new recruit the fundamentals of army life, military traditions, and essential survival skills. During army infantry training, one learns how to march, dress, and groom oneself properly as well as how to do tasks as a team. There are several task-specific instructors and drill instructors who oversee each training process. The training of a recruit split down into different stages, and the commander of the training company is crucial in developing the soldiers of the future.

Phase I

This phase starts off the training programme and lasts for one week. During this week, recruits are given official admission paperwork and undergo a medical checkup. Additionally, they get their kit and are given maintenance instructions. During this initial week of training, recruits also become familiar with the Kumaon Regimental Centre.

Phase II

The second phase of recruit training is four weeks of basic training followed by a break of two weeks off for the candidates. Numerous physical exercises are included in the basic training, including marching, drill, route-marching, weapon instruction, and physical training. They might also participate in obstacle courses and compete in sports, like running. The second phase of training is classroom instruction where candidates learn the fundamentals of weapon assembly, navigation, and tactical operations.

Phase III

This phase lasts 15 weeks and entails advanced training with a set daily schedule. Recruits attend lectures on military culture and discipline. In the field under simulated settings, they also learn how to maintain their equipment properly and handle their weapons effectively. They also learn about national challenges involving defence, security, and military strategies like camouflage, concealment, and patrols. All the abilities that recruits have learned during the first three phases are tested by their instructors.

Phase IV

Operational training takes place over the course of the final two weeks. Combat-patrolling, route-marching, cross-country navigation, and tactical drills are all part of this training. The fourth phase of the training plan, which marks the end of fundamental training, includes a concluding graduation ceremony. After completing this stage, applicants join the various battalions of the Kumaon Regiment as soldiers.

The year, 1953, passed and Shaitan continued to be a company commander. A new year arrived with new changes in the regiment. In 1954, two new units of the regiment were to be given regimental colours. A few months before the ceremony, the commandant Lt Col MR Yadava was replaced after completion of his tenure at KRC by Lt Col NK Sinha, who just completed his tenure as the commanding officer of 4 Kumaon at Balnoi in Jammu & Kashmir, was handed over the baton of the commandant as the 24th commandant of the prestigious Kumaon Regimental Centre, on April 18.

In May 1954 Shaitan and other officers were due to get their annual leave which Shaitan usually availed of one month. However, this time, Shaitan applied for a two-month-long leave in May. His leave was readily sanctioned from May 24 to July 22. But he stayed in the centre for a few days before going home. On May 25, he received a letter stating that he had been granted permanent commission, for which he had applied this year. Now SS-16229 was no longer his service number, it was now IC-6400, a number which is registered in the golden letters of the Indian Army's history.

His short service, which was to end in November 1954, was converted to permanent service. It meant another 20-plus years of service. During this period only he was permanently transferred to 13 Kumaon on papers. The 6th Kumaon Regiment was no longer his parent unit, it was now the 13th Kumaon Regiment.

After this, Shaitan proceeded on leave. Shaitan had planned the leave because his agricultural land in his native Rajasthan was affected by adverse weather conditions triggering a drought, which resulted in crop failure. Maj Gen Vishwanathan, a colleague of Shaitan Singh from the Kumaon Regimental Centre, remembers Shaitan as a very pleasant gentleman and a conscientious officer. He also recalls how once Shaitan took leave in the summer while posted at KRC. He visited his family to help them during the drought.

Shaitan returned to the KRC in July during the monsoon season, during which the centre became more beautiful and scenic.

During this period centre prepared for the colours-presentation ceremony for the two new member battalions of the regiment. The regiment was honoured to welcome the new units as well as its colonel of the regiment was awarded the Padma Bhushan. Hence, the event was going to be a major celebratory occasion.

Two additional battalions had joined the Kumaon family in February 1953: the 4th Gwalior Infantry, commanded by Lt Col

JR Mehra, and the Indore Infantry, commanded by Lt Col Ram Singh, a Mewari officer who subsequently rose to the position of regimental centre commandant. These two Madhya Bharat (Central India) Forces units were initially associated with the Rajput Regiment following the restructuring and union of the armed forces of the princely states with the Indian Army. By May 1953, they had been redesignated, with the 4th Gwalior Infantry becoming the Kumaon Regiment's 14th battalion and the Indore Infantry its 15th battalion. The 14th battalion adopted the suffix "Gwalior", while the 15th battalion added "Indore" to its name. This was possible because they were allowed to maintain ties to their past. On Kumaon Day in 1954, Shaitan was part of the event preparations but could not attend the ceremony as he was called up for the Platoon Weapons Officer Course at Infantry School, Mhow. Kumaon Day is observed each year on October 27 to mark the renaming of the 19th Hyderabad Regiment to Kumaon Regiment.

On Kumaon Day 1954, Lt Gen Thimayya officially welcomed the two new battalions into the Kumaon family by presenting them with the regimental flags (colours) at Ranikhet.

Platoon Weapons Officer Course

It was September and Shaitan still served as the training company commander when he received a letter to attend the Platoon Weapons Officer Course, Serial No. 17. On September 15, the course was scheduled to begin. A day before the start of the course, Shaitan set out on his trip to Mhow. Ratlam, a town in Madhya Bharat (now Madhya Pradesh) and a major railway station of the region, was his stop. There, he ran into his closest friend Capt Mal Singh and a few other officers, including Capt H.N. Sur of his own parent unit, 13 Kumaon. Together, they set out on their journey to Mhow. The officers were given accommodation when they arrived at the infantry school. Shaitan and Mal Singh decided to stay in the same room.

After orientation for the course's planned events, the course officially began the following day. Shaitan was surprised to learn that the course's senior instructor was Maj Sangram Singh from Jodhpur, who was his senior in Kotah Umed Infantry. Maj Sangram Singh had lately been assigned to 5 Jat and was that time serving as a senior instructor at the Infantry School. A Kumaoni who commanded the 3 Kumaon Rifles, Lt Col Gurbans Singh Bal was the commandant of the Weapons Wing.

The course was designed to enhance the young officers' knowledge of how to use and operate weapons at the platoon level and develop their skills and experience. There were two platoons made up of the course's strength. Most of the candidates were either young captains or subalterns. Capt K.S. Gurung was assigned control of one platoon, and Capt Rishal Singh was assigned control of the other. The 75-day course had theory lectures, practical classes, and examinations at the final stages. Shaitan was acquainted with Capt Ajit Singh, an officer in the Jammu & Kashmir Infantry who had received the Vir Chakra for his valiant actions in Skardu while serving with the J&K State Forces in 1948. Capt Ajit Singh was the lone recipient of any gallantry award in the course.

On November 30, 1954, the course culminated with a group photograph of instructors and candidates was clicked. Shaitan obtained excellent grades, but he missed the instructor's grade by a few points.

On December 5, Shaitan returned to the centre and got involved in the training activities of the recruits. The year rolled to 1955. As a company commander, Shaitan was still shaping and training the Kumaon Regiment's future. He had an ordinary year, although one of the few events that happened was his substantive promotion to the rank of captain on November 25, 1955. He had lost five years of seniority due to his service in the state forces, which led to promotions being given out later.

Although he received the promotion to the position of acting captain in June 1953, it took him an additional two and a half years to receive the substantive rank.

Also, in this calendar year, he didn't get any kind of annual leave. He couldn't visit his home on account of his service commitments. I came across a poignant gesture by Shaitan, when he got to know that he wasn't going on leave. He wrote a letter to his brother Surajbhan and attached a photograph, on which "With love to Suraj" was written. A part of the letter reads: "You couldn't see me this year, so I'm sending this letter with my recent photograph in uniform so that you could see me."

Shaitan And Shareef

Lt Gen Guru Bakshi, a former director general of the infantry and NCC, joined the Kumaon Regiment in 1956 as a freshly commissioned officer. He recalls an incident from the same year. His narration of it was something like this: "When Maj Gen Bikram Singh, GOC of the 25th Infantry Division, landed at the centre one day, the officers hosted a party that night at the centre's mess, with Maj Gen Bikram Singh as the special guest. As the party started, Lt Col N.K. Sinha, the commandant, was introducing his officers to the general. One by one, he began introducing them. Maj Mohar Singh, Maj T.S. Samra, Maj S.C. Suri, Capt N.A. Sallick, (who was Vir Chakra recipient and a hero of the war of 1947-1948), and Lt P.C. Mehta and others were among the officers present.

"Sir, I'm Captain Sheriff," said an officer from 6 Kumaon before it was Shaitan's turn. Shaitan had previously held the position of adjutant for 6 Kumaon in Shillong, and Bikram Singh was the brigade commander at 181 Independent Brigade Group, Shillong. Shaitan had already begun to feel shy and hesitant because of his name. However, when it was Shaitan's turn, both he and Bikram Singh recognised each other as they had interacted frequently due to their respective appointments. After shaking hands with the general, he introduced himself as Capt Shaitan Singh in a firm voice. Maj Gen Bikram chuckled and responded, "We have some Shaitan and Shareef officers in the regiment," before adding, "You still couldn't get your name changed, son. I recall that you requested that your name be changed on a particular occasion. But keep in mind that your name is perfect.'' Because of his unique personality, Gen Bikram Singh often used humour to make his colleagues smile. He was a man with a steely exterior and a tender interior.

Shaitan and Sheriff lived in adjacent rooms in the officers' mess, and because of their contrasting names, they were frequently teased. The most prevalent remark was that Shaitan was Shareef and Sheriff was Shaitan, although this was untrue. Capt Sheriff was an extremely capable officer who also had a humorous side.

A Trainee and His Fond Memories

In 2022, at a reunion event of a Kumaon battalion, I happened to meet an elderly veteran who had trained under Maj Shaitan Singh. It was a stroke of luck for me because I had long desired to meet people who had first-hand experiences with Shaitan Singh. Honorary Captain Chamu Singh Mehra was enlisted into the Kumaon Regiment, in December 1955 at a very young age, was someone I had the opportunity to get to know. Despite being recruited in December, he recalls that he received his Army order and enrolled on January 24, 1956. Mehra said, "I didn't know anything when I arrived at the centre. It was also the first time I left my home. How the world functioned was unfamiliar to me. Capt Shaitan Singh, the company commander, greeted us the following day.

"In his speech, (Shaitan Singh) Sahab said: 'Bachho, bade aaram se training karna; mausam thanda hai, apna khayal karna.

Yaha jo anghethi hai, usse jala kar rakhna aur raat ko aaram se sona.' ['Boys, train with ease; the weather is cold, take care of yourself. Keep the coal stove burning and sleep comfortably at night.']"

He has memories of the kits, particularly the blankets. He claims they were quite dated and that most of them had received multiple blankets to keep them warm.

When asked about his training, Mehra recalled being in the Charlie Company under Shaitan Singh, who would frequently visit to oversee the training sessions. Alpha, Bravo, and Delta companies each had their own training area in Dhulikhet, whereas Mehra's company had a separate training area. He said they used to go to the Dhulikhet ground following four weeks of basic training. Most of the recruits were illiterate or had minimal education. Back then, even simple commands like "left turn" or "right turn" were given in the English language.

Since most of the recruits had trouble following the instructions, Shaitan led them carefully. On occasions, he would even interrupt the instructor and say: "Let me speak to this boy and instruct them by demonstrating right and left by holding their hands." Shaitan made learning things extremely simple for the new recruits. Shaitan claimed that there was nothing special in his command. However, the officer never let his men suffer and in turn, it made him special in the eyes. He always stood for those under his command and never chastised his men or flaunted his rank. He cherished them.

He recalls the time when drill instructors would yell at the new recruits and would even slap them for making mistakes. Shaitan prohibited such behaviour and warned the instructors when they violated his instructions on this issue. He always emphasised teaching and training the recruits by demonstrating things rather than resort to corporal punishment. Often, Shaitan himself took it on himself to instruct the recruits.

Mehra recalls Shaitan as a very gentle and modest man who would often tell instructors: "These boys have come straight from their homes leaving their families, and you're scolding them here. You should refrain from doing this and treat them well." Mehra says Shaitan never reprimanded anyone or spoke harshly to them. He was extremely kind and humble.

Hony Capt Chamu Singh Mehra enlisted in the 6 Kumaon in 1956 as a sepoy and served with his battalion as a naik in the Walong sector in the North-East Frontier Agency (NEFA) during the 1962 India-China war - the war which also claimed the life of his beloved training company commander Shaitan Singh. Shaitan had trained many recruits who took part in various operations during the wars of 1962, 1965, 1971 and the counter-insurgency operations in the Naga Hills and Mizoram.

The Quartermaster

In 1956, the summer was pleasant in Ranikhet. On May 20, Shaitan was relieved from his post as company commander and given the new position of quartermaster of the Kumaon Regimental Centre. He learned a lot from the appointment, which benefited him immensely. He had to handle everything as the QM of the centre — from transportation to supplies and munitions. He handled his new responsibilities deftly even though it was a demanding task.

He had already applied for his annual leave to travel home after two months on the new appointment. It was already two years when he last saw his family. After a long period, he was delighted to be able to be granted leave to spend some time with his family and friends from July 16 to September 13. Shaitan travelled to Jodhpur, where he with his brothers and his son, Narpat, who were enrolled in college and a school respectively. He then travelled to Banasar, where he spent most of his leave. Midway through September, he went back to the KRC and resumed his duties as the centre's quartermaster. He ran into some faces that were unfamiliar this time at the centre: Capt Raghunath V. Jatar and Capt Vishwanathan. Originally from Kumaon 13, Jatar 'would to be' Shaitan's good friend. The young captain was the recently appointed training company commander at the centre, and this was Shaitan's first meeting with him.

It was March 1957, and spring had started. Shaitan who planned to send his son, Narpat, to Mussoorie to a missionary-run boarding school received a letter from home stating that his son residing at boarding school in Jodhpur had contracted smallpox and was staying at his brother-in-law's place. Shaitan got worried knowing this but he also received good news about the birth of his nephew. After receiving this information, Shaitan regularly used to write letters to his brother-in-law giving instructions on how to treat Narpat and when to take him to hospital. This went on till Narpat completely recovered.

In one such letter he wrote:

My dear Mool Singh ji Sahib

Jai Shri Kishan

Very kind of you for the letter which unfortunately I could not reply earlier. I am well here and wish you all the best.

From your letters it appears that Narpat is still with you. Please do not keep him with you and send him or get him admitted in some isolation hospital. I am worried Ghanshyam or Mahendra might be affected by it. Hope you will kindly do this much.
You gave me the happiest news about the new arrival and that too a son to Sun (Suraj). How wonderful it is– God is really very great. Please let me know how the baby is progressing. How is Mrs Suraj? Hope she is fit enough to take care of the baby. Has Suraj come? I am sure you must have informed my mother also. She will be most happy to hear this much awaited/wanted news. Please inform Hem Singh ji or much I would like, to be informed is Mrs Hem Singh ji.

It would not be any exaggeration if I say that it was all because of you and sister that everyone is happy today? How can I ever forget today? How can I ever forget your benevolence? You are a great asset to me and my whole family.

Have you sent the money to Suraj & Lal & Co? How is everybody in Jodhpur?

Now about Narpat's schooling, I have written to the principal and am awaiting his reply. In the meanwhile, if it takes long, Narpat may be sent back to school.

What have you thought of Ugam's marriage proposal? Uncertain days are fast approaching and you never know what happens in the near future so it would be much better if things are sorted out earliest.

How is sister? Please convey my Ashirvad to her and love to Ghanshyam and Mahendra. My regards to Mrs Suraj.

Jai Shri I ji

Sincerely yours

Shaitan Singh

Later in the same month following an order from his seniors, Shaitan, the quartermaster, sent a notification to all the companies in the centre instructing them to submit all misfired bullet cases every Monday and fired cases every Friday. The instructions also included that a proper record of these cases be kept. Misfired and fired cases were delivered to the Central Ordnance Depot in Jabalpur on the first Monday and last Friday of every month respectively. Unfortunately, on April 24, the COD Jabalpur reported receiving a box containing 59 bicat strips, which are used to store ammunition, instead of empty cases. It was Shaitan's duty to thoroughly inspect each box before sending it to Jabalpur. Now, according to the complaint, it was the quartermaster's mistake.

On June 3, a court of inquiry was set up to investigate the matter. Shaitan had never witnessed a CoI before. It was the first and the only CoI he faced in his career. Maj S.C. Suri presided over the court, which also had Lt P.C. Mehta and Sub Maj Shyamu Mall, VrC, as members. There were seven witnesses who testified in Capt Shaitan Singh's favour, and not one of them blamed QM. The CoI later determined that the box containing the bicat strips was not sent from Kumaon Regimental Centre, and, thus, Shaitan was not at fault.

Shaitan took his annual leave following the CoI. He was again designated as a training officer, on June 13, while he was on leave. He took over as a training officer on July 6. The appointment of the new commandant occurred at the centre shortly after he returned from leave, which was another significant event. On July 11, Lt Col N.K. Sinha handed Lt Col Ram Singh the reins of the KRC. A veteran of the Second World War, Lt Col Ram Singh was an accomplished officer. He began his military career in the Mewar State Forces and served in the Second World War and Operation Polo before enlisting in the Indian Army. He was chosen to serve as the 15 Kumaon's commanding officer after the Indore Infantry was merged into the Kumaon Regiment. Lt Col Ram Singh passed away in 2019 at the age of 102.

Shaitan Singh held the position of training officer till he received the transfer order to move to the headquarters General Officer Commanding Assam as General Staff Officer-3. On October 16, 1957, a dining-out party was organised for Shaitan in the presence of the commandant and his other colleagues at the KRC. Little did he know that one day, a ground where recruits train would be named after him and that he and his soldiers' belongings would become a main feature of the regimental centre's museum. After a sincere four-year relationship with the Kumaon Regimental Centre, an emotional Shaitan left the installation, on October 18, 1957.

References

1. Documents of Major Shaitan Singh, PVC
2. Letters of Major Shaitan Singh, PVC
3. Interview with Honorary Captain Chamu Singh Mehra (retd)
4. Interview with Brigadier Raghunath V. Jatar (retd)
5. Interview with Commandant Prithvi Singh (retd)
6. Interview with Mr Narpat Singh
7. Telephonic conversation with Maj Gen Vishwanathan (retd)
8. Telephonic conversation with late Colonel Narendra Kumar, PVSM, KC, AVSM, FRGS (retd)
9. Telephonic conversation with Lt Gen Guru Bakshi (retd)
10. Website: https://indianarmy.nic.in/

❑

Operation Raji

The Staff Captain

Captain Shaitan Singh

This chapter shares the story of Operation Raji and Shaitan Singh's tenure in the Naga Hills with HQ GOC Assam and 23 Infantry Division during the peak of insurgency in the state. He served as the general staff officer-3 and looked after updating and gathering intelligence related to the counter-insurgency operations. He remained in the area for three years and did his Junior Command Course during this tenure.

A New Appointment

October 19, 1957, was the date. After leaving the Kathgodam railway station, Capt Shaitan Singh travelled to Dimapur, where he arrived on October 23 and lodged at a transit camp. The following day, he was supposed to report to Kohima, where he travelled by road transport because there was no available railway line. When Shaitan arrived in Kohima, he went to the GOC Assam headquarters to report after being named as the GSO-3 (Intelligence and Operations). He was formally named the GSO-3 of the division headquarters on October 25. His duties included reporting, monitoring ongoing operations, and updating the intelligence.

The Assam Division was the only Indian Army division at the time that oversaw most of the northeastern states. The division was given the task of eradicating the ongoing Naga insurgency, which started in the mid-1950s, and preserving peace in the Naga Hills. Shaitan, with 6 Kumaon, had already worked as part of the division earlier and his unit had already carried out several anti-insurgency operations.

The Naga Revolt

The Naga problem first surfaced in the mid-1950s. The Naga people comprise several Naga tribes, who can sometimes be very distinct from one another in their dialects, customs, etc. Even their geographical range and terrain also vary. The Naga tribes had lived in near-complete isolation in remote areas for centuries. They follow a simple way of life and have charming customs and traditions. They are known to be fierce fighters who are native of India's eastern frontier. Today, the Naga people have their home state - Nagaland, which is made up of the Naga Hills and the Tuensang division. It was once a part of the North-East Frontier Agency (now Arunachal Pradesh). Naga communities also extend to Manipur state and Myanmar across the international border.

In the earlier days of the British Raj, a few of the Naga tribes engaged in headhunting. It was their rapacious excursions into the Assam plains that brought about the first encounters with them. Administrative posts had to be set up in their region, and punitive expeditions had to be launched to deter the tribesmen from raiding the Assam plains.

After that, if the Nagas maintained peace, the British left them alone. The Nagas' innate desire to maintain their unique identity was strengthened by their seclusion, and when the Simon Commission visited India, in 1929, they indicated a desire to be exempt from the reforms that were being discussed. The Naga Hills was designated as an "excluded area" in the 1935 Government of India Act, which gave it provincial autonomy.

Even after Independence, specific protections for Naga social practices, customary law, and the ownership and transfer of land and its resources were incorporated into India's Constitution. However, this did not appease the more aggressive members within the Naga tribespeople. Instead, they demanded total independence from India. Angami Zapu Phizo served as the Naga movement's leader, and among other Naga leaders at that time, he gained support, and his stature grew. By 1954, he started an open rebellion against the Union of India.

The rebels established a parallel rival government in March 1956, assembled their own army (the Naga Home Guard), and carred out violent attacks on government employees and security personnel. The Indian Army was summoned after the civil authorities failed to handle the rebellion. As a result of the prior work done by 6 Kumaon and others, a counter-insurgency plan to quell the rebellion — "Operation Raji" — was initiated.

On October 24, 1956, the division's 17 Rajput unit suffered one fatality while it conducted an operation in the operational area.

Under the command of Lt Col R.K. Yadava, the 15 Kumaon left Jaipur at the end of November 1956 to join the 201 Infantry Brigade and participate in anti-rebel operations. Along with conducting extensive patrolling, the battalion had to man critical posts, such as Merangkong in Ao territory, Wakching in Konyak area, milestone 53 on the Jorhat-Mokokchung route, and the Tuli Camp.

It was difficult to deal with the hostile Nagas. Even the peace-inclined tribespeople had tremendous sympathy for the rebels. The rebels had advanced notice of the troops' arrival, and their hiding places were hidden deep within the forests. Some of the rebels were ex-servicemen from the Assam Rifles and Assam Regiment, who either defected or were discharged from these organisations. They were armed with a variety of basic muzzle-loaders, shotguns, pistols, sten guns, light machine guns, and a few Japanese weaponry left over from the Second World War. Thousands of Japanese perished from wounds and illnesses when they withdrew from Kohima and Imphal. At that time, many Nagas took custody of their arsenal and maintained them.

It was Time tor Operations

The 15 Kumaon encountered the enemy for the first time on December 10 when shotguns and light machine guns fired at their station at Milestone 53 during the night. However, when a combat patrol was dispatched to deal with the rebels, they escaped. The battalion's first significant success occurred on December 24, 1956. On that day, a two-platoon patrol caught a "general" of the Naga Home Guard (NHG) along with 14 other insurgents at Kanching. They also seized a shotgun and a significant amount of cash from them.

The division had some initial success against the insurgents till one of its battalions suffered its first fatalities, on January 5, 1957, on the Amguri-Mokokchung road at Milestone 23. A sepoy was killed, and another was wounded in an attack on the water point close to the platoon position. However, by the end of the month, 127 insurgents surrendered. They claimed to be tired of fighting and wanted to become law-abiding citizens. At the 15 Kumaon headquarters in Merangkong, a ceremony was held to mark the rebels' surrender.

The battalion moved to Mokokchung in the last week of May after holding positions at Chungtia, Longchang, and Lungkam. Although the tribes the unit had fought were different, the practice persisted there as well.

Although our troops' actions in the Naga Hills were largely successful, the terrain and the restrictions placed on them prevented them from completely suppressing rebel activity. The rebels persisted in harassing the locals, extorting food and cash from them, and kidnapping or murdering anyone who was seen as aiding the Indian Army and government officials. The Nagas typically resided in tiny communities, each with a collection of huts that was separate from the others. The rebels successfully escaped by the time word of a raid on a village reached them before the soldiers could get there. Thus, security was increased in the communities. A plan for grouping involved the construction of larger villages and the relocation of the residents from the neighbouring villages.

Beginning in October, the 192 Infantry Brigade took control of the 15 Kumaon, which later in the month relieved the 2/9 Gorkha Rifles at Sapotimi with stations at Tichi Pami, Chare, the Dikhu bridge, Aichi Sagami, Yangli, and Sirohoto.

The 13 Kumaon, which returned from Kashmir, had spent minimal time at Ramgarh before relocating to Ranchi in February 1955. After that, the battalion relocated to Ferozepur in June. They subsequently worked for a while at Fazilka and the Sulemanki Headworks. Then the unit received an order to go to Naga Hills, and on September 29, 1957, they arrived at the Manipur Road under the command of Lt Col N.S. Krishna. By October 6, they had relieved 3 Bihar and joined the 181 Infantry Brigade. Their destination was Wokha, northeast of Dimapur.

The battalion established various posts with a size ranging from a platoon to a company, the most significant being at Koio, Yekhum, Kotsenyu, and Lungsa. The battalion had its headquarters in the Lotha area at Wokha. The bulk of the battalion's transportation took place at Kohima, near the division headquarters, while their rear dump was located at the Dimapur airport. Till now Capt Shaitan Singh of 13 Kumaon had also joined the division headquarters as GSO-3. Although the 201 Infantry Brigade took control of 13 Kumaon in December, their area of duty remained the same.

Shaitan had begun performing his duties and was busy with the ongoing operations. He participated in this operation with two units of his own regiment, one of which being his own parent unit. Shaitan had visited his unit at times during the operations. There, he met Maj Gulab Singh, a senior from the Kotah Umed Infantry, and Capt Mukut Singh. The three became good friends.

Junior Command Course

In December, Shaitan received a letter to report to attend the Junior Command Course, Serial No. 23 at the Infantry School, Mhow. As he had been granted permanent commission in 1954, it was time for him to attend the course. The JCC, which was based on British military concepts of warfare, is compressive and intended to teach medium-grade commanders operational leadership. It was an intermediate-level course created to prepare officers for subunit-/company-level command, staff, and instructional assignments.

Majors or captains can enrol in this 13-week course three times a year, which is a requirement for middle-grade officers to be promoted majors. The student officers are led up to command level through this training. They are trained to take over command of a company strength subunit, which is suitable for medium-grade staff positions. Student officers are primarily trained at the battalion level under the brigade and division structure to gain a solid understanding of staff responsibilities, operations of war doctrine, and counter-insurgency environments.

Shaitan along with Capt Mukut Singh of 13 Kumaon moved to the Manipur Road from Kohima, and from there to Mhow via Ujjain. They reached Mhow on December 22 while Shaitan's schoolfriend Capt Bijai Singh, who belonged to the Punjab Regiment, arrived a day earlier. Bijai learned that Shaitan would also be attending this course. He requested a room for himself and Shaitan from the administration.

When Shaitan arrived at the Infantry School's housing facility and learned that he would be sharing a room with Bijai, he immediately went to the administrative facility to request that his room be changed. He was aware that Bijai was a mischievous individual and very different from him, and he also knew that they couldn't stay together. Anand Kanwar, the daughter of Lt Col Bijai Singh, recalls that Shaitan managed to get his room changed.

The course started. During the orientation, the student officers were briefed about the course's schedule and events by the senior instructor, Lt Col Sagat Singh. Sagat Singh went on to become a general in the Indian Army for his notable participation in the liberation of Goa, 1967 India-China clashes in Sikkim, and later in the 1971 Bangladesh Liberation War. He held many commands and staff appointments throughout his career.

Anand Kanwar, who remembers her father's association with Shaitan Singh, says, "Major Shaitan and my father both had totally different personalities. While participating in an evening game of football, Shaitan once suffered an injury. He went to his room and was relaxing on his bed when my father, who was not aware of his injury, entered and jumped on him, unintentionally aggravating his injury. Shaitan was so kind and considerate that he told Bijai about his pain and asked him to stop doing similar things in the future without additional words."

The course came to an end on March 22. As it was customary, a group photograph was taken. Shaitan passed the course with a fine grade. However, he was told that he was shy and lacked assertiveness in his leadership and needed to improve his self-confidence.

I was honoured to visit the exact same place where the group photograph was taken.

Just after the course, Shaitan was recalled to the division. He immediately travelled to Kohima with a halt at Lucknow. The leave for which he had applied was postponed by two weeks. In the meantime, Shaitan wrote to his brother Surajbhan Singh. 'I'm planning to come [home] on annual leave. I hope to reach Jodhpur on April 10 or 11, that is, a week later. If you receive my letter in time, find a suitable bungalow-type house for me. I want to stay in Jodhpur during my leave. Secondly, if you are preparing for exams, then please don't go out to find a house. Please don't waste your time if your exams are in May.' His leave was later approved by the GOC HQ at Kohima. Shaitan then left for Jodhpur from Kohima. Again, this time he took his annual leave during the summer.

During the leave this time, he stayed in Jodhpur instead of his home in the village. He had already asked his wife to come to Jodhpur with their son. The family stayed in a bungalow called "Colonel Jawahar Singh ji ka Bungalow", near the railway line on the Risala Road. He got his son, Narpat, admitted to a government boarding school far from home in Ajmer, instead of getting him admitted to a school in Mussoorie, which he planned in the previous year. His leave was over on June 5, and he went back to join duty at Kohima.

When he reached Kohima after five and a half months, he found several changes there, and the Army made steady progress in the counter-insurgency operations.

The 15 Kumaon had returned to Merangkong by the middle of February 1958. Upon learning of a hostile camp nearby, a company-sized patrol was dispatched. The troops dealt a serious blow to the insurgents. They killed and injured a few of them, captured some weapons and ammunition.

The Naga rebels' propensity to regularly move their area of operation presented a significant challenge in dealing with them. They would shift from one location to another making it difficult for the Army to engage them. To counter this issue, the Army was left with the only solution of cleaning up the entire tribal territory. On April 24, the Army launched "Operation Jhoom" to meet this objective.

To relieve the 2 Jat, the 13 Kumaon had begun to relocate to a different location a week earlier. By April 20, the company posts at Maromi, Lungkam, and Ratomi had been replaced by Lumami as the battalion headquarters.

Both 13 and 15 Kumaon participated in the operation. The operation, which lasted till May 3, was successful in finding and eliminating a few hostile Naga camps and rebels' hiding places. The senior rebel leaders managed to escape but several other insurgents were captured.

Soon after "Operation Jhoom", it was time for the 15 Kumaon to get a break. Gaya was to be their next station, and their advance party left Jorhat on May 15. But the Ao tribe kept the 15 Kumaon busy till the very end of their stay in the Naga Hills. Patrolling and raids continued, with the one on the

Lt Col Hem Singh

Lt Col Hem Singh, OBI

Rajput School, Chopasni

Labhshankar Football Challenge Cup Tournament, 1942.
(L to R) *On Ground: Ajab Singh, Chhotu Singh*
On Chairs: *Bhikam Singh, Mr Madan Lal, AP Cox, Ganpat Singh, Randheer Singh*
Standing: *Devi Singh, Shaitan Singh, Mool Singh, Bijai Singh*

Colonel Mohan Singh

Marwar Football League.
(L to R) On Ground: *Prem Singh Gehlot, Bahadur Singh*
On Chairs: *Shaitan Singh, Shivdutt, Col Kalyan Singh, Brig Jabar Singh, Col Dungar Singh, Roop Singh, Randhir Singh.*
Standing: *Bajran Singh, Bhoor Singh, Sardar Khan, Maj Ramdan Singh, Moti Singh, Chandan Mal Dugar*

Durga Horse Football Team
(L to R) On Ground: *Hari Singh, —*
On Chairs: *—, —, Col Mohan Singh, Randhir Singh, Shaitan Singh*
Standing: Nawal Singh, Bhoor Singh, Bahadur Singh, Shivdutt

SOC Shaitan Singh, Durga Horse

SOC Shaitan Singh and SOC Hari Singh

2/Lt Shaitan Singh, Jodhpur Sardar Infantry

SOC Shaitan Singh with his horse

(L to R) SOC Shaitan Singh, SOC Durga Das, SOC Hari Singh

Officers' Supplementary Course No. 3, OTS Poona 1949

Officers and JCOs of 6 Kumaon, Shillong, 1952
(L to R) Sitting: 8 JCOs, On Chairs: Lt Jaswant Singh, —, Maj PH Honawar, —, 2-IC, Lt Col Kaman Singh, MVC, Sub Maj Arjun Singh, Maj HS Bolina, VrC, —, Lt Lakha Singh, —
—, 2/Lt Shaitan Singh and 12 Officers and JCOs

Officers and JCOs of Kotah Umed Infantry with GOC 19 Infantry

2/Lt Shaitan Singh,
Kotah Umed Infantry

Captain Shaitan Singh,
Kumaon Regimental
Centre

2/Lt Shaitan Singh, 6 Kumaon

Captain Shaitan Singh

2/Lt Shaitan Singh escorting Maj Gen Mahadeo Singh, DSO

Officers of 6 Kumaon, 26 January 1952

General Intelligence Course for Officers Serial 14, MHOW

3-Inch mortar course, MHOW, 1951

Platoon Weapons Officer Course-17, MHOW, 1954

Captain Shaitan Singh with his friends

Captain Shaitan Singh and Captain Magni Ram

Captain Shaitan Singh with officers of 23 Infantry Division

Lt Gen Bikram Singh

Captain Shaitan Singh, 13 Kumaon

Junior Command Course, 1958

Officers of 13 Kumaon, Ambala. ***(L to R) Sitting:*** *Maj G Halgali, Maj HN Sur, Maj HS Dhingra, Gen KS Thimayya, Lt Col BS Chand, VrC, Maj Mukut Singh, Maj Jaswant Singh.* ***Standing:*** *2/Lt Prem Kumar, Capt Shaitan Singh, Capt HS Chauhan, Lt BS Lamba, 2/Lt RK Khanna, 2/Lt attached from AOC*

Officers and ladies of 13 Kumaon with Gen KS Thimayya at Ambala

Gen KS Thimayya meeting officers of 13 Kumaon

Officers of 13 Kumaon with Gen KS Thimayya at Ambala ***(L to R) Standing:*** *Maj HN Sur, Lt Col SY Munshi, Maj HS Dhingra, Maj Mukut Singh, Capt Shaitan Singh, Maj Halgali, Maj Jaswant Singh, 2/Lt Ramesh Khanna, Lt BS Lamba, 2/Lt Prem Kumar, Capt HS Chauhan, AOC 2/Lt* ***Sitting:*** *Lt Col BS Chand VrC and Gen Thimayya*

Capt Shaitan Singh escorting Lt Gen K Bahadur Singh, Ambala

Officers of 13 Kumaon
***(L to R)** Lt Prem Kumar, Lt Ramesh Khanna, Capt Shaitan Singh, Maj Halgali, Capt ED Wayte, Maj GN Sinha*

Officers of 13 Kumaon in Goa Liberation (L to R) Maj GN Sinha, Maj Mukut Singh, Maj KP Kandeth, MC, Lt Col BS Chand, VrC, Maj Jaswant Singh. Standing: Capt HS Chauhan, —, Lt PM Wakhle, Capt Shaitan Singh, Capt DD Saklani , Lt BS Lamba

***(L to R)** Lt BS Lamba, Capt DD Saklani, Lt PM Wakhle, Capt Shaitan Singh*

Maj Shaitan Singh,
13 Kumaon

13 Kumaon Headquarters at Chushul

International Red Cross team
approaching Rezang La

Lt Col HS Dhingra

Officers climbing up Rezang La

International Red Cross team approaching Rezang La

Retrieval of bodies

Retrieval of bodies, Company Headquarters

Dead body of a soldier

Dead body of a soldier

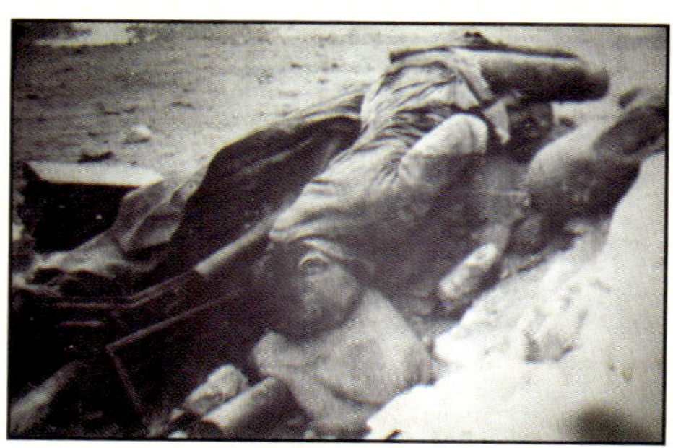

Dead body of a soldier

A destroyed sangar at Rezang La

Lt Col HS Dhingra with Sub Maj Changdi Ram

Sep Ram Chander and a NA with mortal remains of Maj Shaitan Singh, PVC

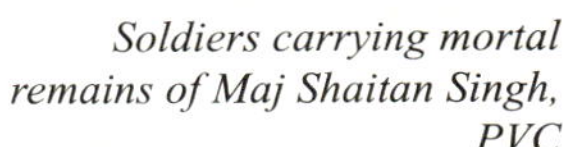

Soldiers carrying mortal remains of Maj Shaitan Singh, PVC

Yaks carrying mortal remains of soldiers at Rezang La

Guard of Honour to Maj Shaitan Singh, PVC at Chushul

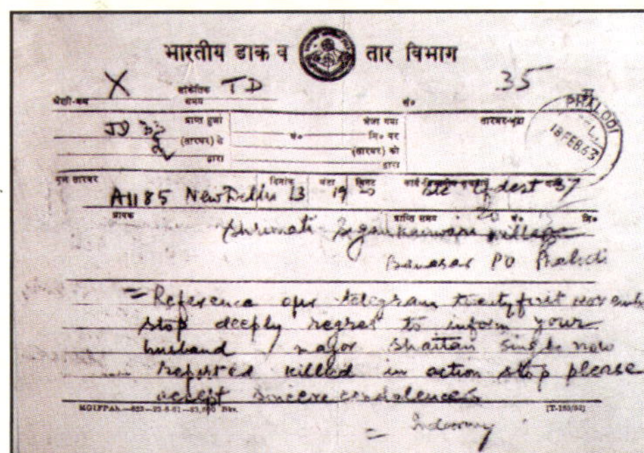

भारतीय डाक व तार विभाग

X TD 35

PHALODI 18 FEB 63

A1185 New Delhi 13 19

Shrimati Sugan Kanwar village Banasar PO Phalodi

= Reference our telegram twenty first November stop deeply regret to inform your husband / Major Shaitan Singh now reported killed in action stop please accept sincere condolences

= Indarmy

Telegram with news of death of Maj Shaitan Singh, PVC

Special Plane carrying mortal remains of Maj Shaitan Singh, PVC

Mr Mohanlal Sukhadia, CM Rajasthan receiving mortal remains of Maj Shaitan Singh, PVC

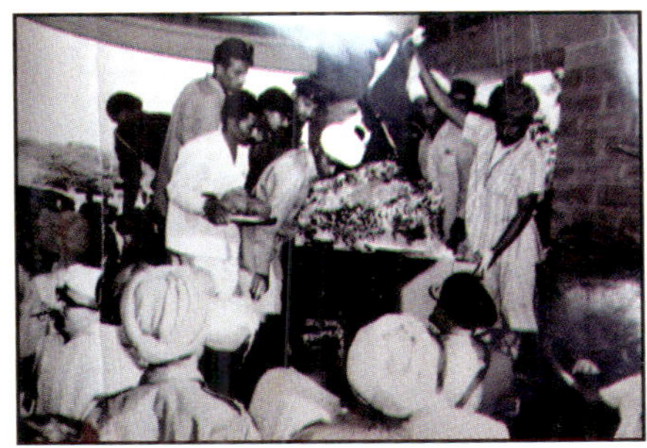

Mr Narpat Singh grieving on his father's mortals

Funeral procession of Maj Shaitan Singh, PVC

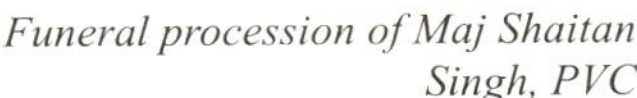

Funeral procession of Maj Shaitan Singh, PVC

Guard of honour to Maj Shaitan Singh, PVC in Jodhpur

Crowd gathered in Jodhpur to bid adieu to Maj Shaitan Singh, PVC

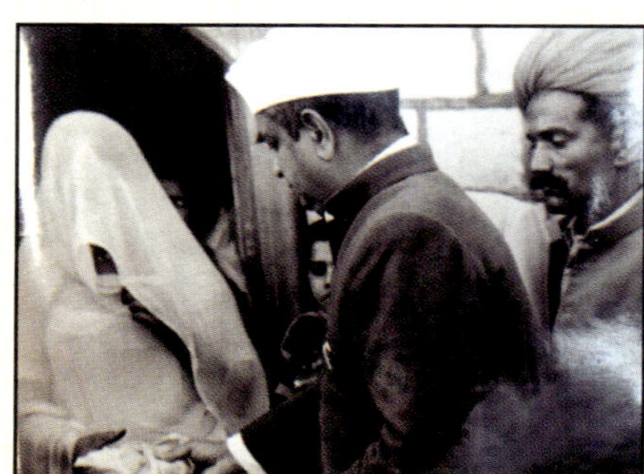

CM Mohanlal Sukhadia presenting help to Mrs Shaitan Singh, in background Sarpanch Udai Singh of Amla

Mass Cremation at Chushul

Mass Cremation at Chushul

Mass Cremation at Chushul

Rezang La Memorial inauguration, 5 August 1963

oung Kashmiri mother with her child whom she has ned Shaitan Singh, after Major Shaitan Singh, hero of Battle of Chushul, whose name has become a byword heroism and sacrifice. Reports have been reaching New hi about a number of cases of new-born babies in the hmir and NEFA areas being named after the Ladakh NEFA heroes who died fighting the Chinese last year.

News paper Clipping

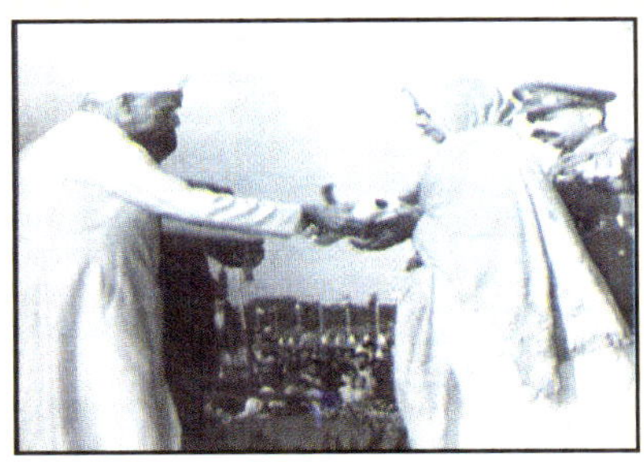

Mrs Shaitan Singh receiving the Paramvir Chakra on behalf of her husband

Lt Col RV Jatar and Mr Narpat Singh during a bust installation in Unit, Jodhpur.

Maj Mal Singh, AC

Jaswant Hostel where Maj Shaitan Singh resided during college days

Place where Maj Shaitan Singh, PVC was cremated

Maj Shaitan Singh, PVC memorial in Jodhpur

Place where Maj Shaitan Singh was mortally wounded at Rezang La

Rezang La Memorial at Chushul after renovation

Author pointing towards Rezang La

Author at Rezang La Memorial on the day of inauguration

Author with Mr Narpat Singh

Author with Brig RV Jatar

Author with Col Shivji Singh

Author with Comdt Prithvi Singh

BA Degree of Maj Shaitan Singh

AGRA UNIVERSITY

Bachelor of Arts

This is to Certify that obtained the Degree of **Bachelor of Arts** in this University in the Examination of 194 , and that he was placed in the Division.

The subjects in which he was examined were General English, Hindi, Economics and History.

Agra University:
The 1947
Vice-Chancellor.

No. 630

BOARD OF HIGH SCHOOL AND INTERMEDIATE EDUCATION, RAJPUTANA (including Ajmer-Merwara), CENTRAL INDIA AND GWALIOR.

Intermediate Examination, 1945.

Roll No. 1088

This is to certify that Shaitan Singh Bhati of Jaswant College, Jodhpur passed the Intermediate Examination held in the month of March/April, 1945, in the following subjects:—

1. English Literature
2. Economics
3. Modern History (Indian - English)
4. Hindi

With distinction in Nil and was placed in the Third Division.

Passed also in the Additional Optional Paper

Madan Mohan Varma
M.A., Rai Bahadur,
Secretary, Board of High School and Intermediate Education, Rajputana (including Ajmer-Merwara), Central India and Gwalior.

AJMER,
June 7, 1945.

Intermediate Exam Certificate

High School Exam Certificate

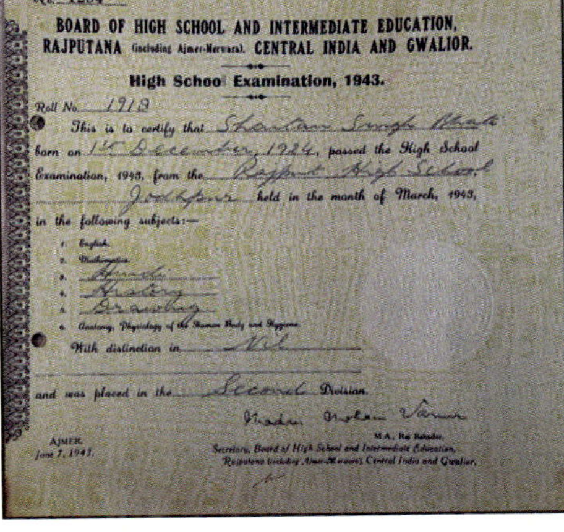

No. 1204

BOARD OF HIGH SCHOOL AND INTERMEDIATE EDUCATION, RAJPUTANA (including Ajmer-Merwara), CENTRAL INDIA AND GWALIOR.

High School Examination, 1943.

Roll No. 1918

This is to certify that Shaitan Singh Bhati born on 1st December, 1924, passed the High School Examination, 1943, from the Rajput High School Jodhpur held in the month of March, 1943, in the following subjects:—

1. English.
2. Mathematics.
3. Hindi
4. History
5. Drawing
6. Anatomy, Physiology of the Human Body and Hygiene.

With distinction in Nil and was placed in the Second Division.

Madan Mohan Varma
M.A., Rai Bahadur,
Secretary, Board of High School and Intermediate Education, Rajputana (including Ajmer-Merwara), Central India and Gwalior.

AJMER,
June 7, 1943.

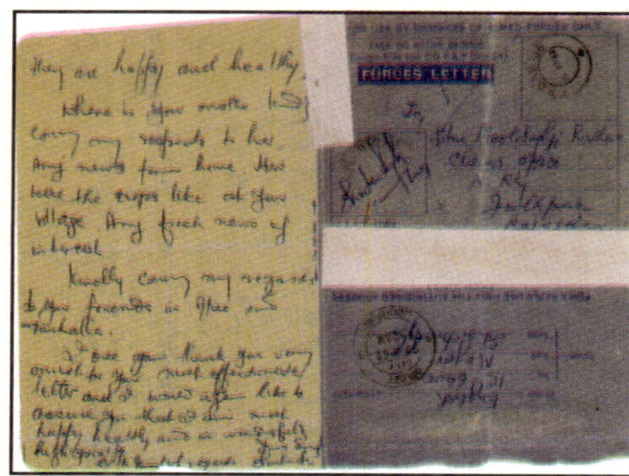

Last letter of Maj Shaitan Singh

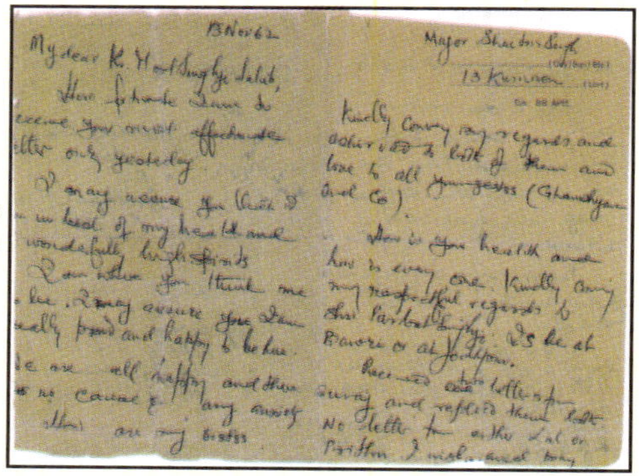

Last letter of Maj Shaitan Singh

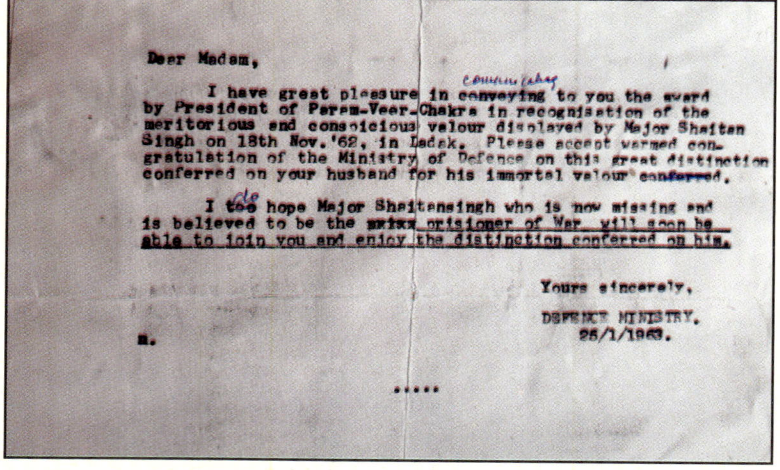

Dear Madam,

I have great pleasure in conveying to you the award by President of Param-Veer-Chakra in recognisation of the meritorious and conspicious valour displayed by Major Shaitan Singh on 18th Nov.'62, in Ladak. Please accept warmed congratulation of the Ministry of Defence on this great distinction conferred on your husband for his immortal valour conferred.

I too hope Major Shaitansingh who is now missing and is believed to be the prisioner of War, will soon be able to join you and enjoy the distinction conferred on him.

Yours sincerely,

DEFENCE MINISTRY.
25/1/1963.

m.

.....

A telegram with news of Maj Shaitan Singh being conferred PVC

EXTRA-ORDINARY

प्रजा सेवक

राष्ट्रीय साप्ताहिक

सत्य मेव जयते

भारत के महान योद्धा मेजर शैतान सिंह का आज शाम को कागा में दाह–संस्कार होगा

बजे हवाई जहाज के मैदान से शव यात्रा शुरू होगी

A Newspaper clipping

Registered No. J. 141

Forward Times

THIS IS PARAM VIR CHAKRA MAJOR Shaitan Singh SPECIAL NUMBER

OUR HOLI SPECIAL

BOOK ADVERTISEMENTS EARLY
RATES ON BACK PAGE

Published from Olympic Cinema Building Jodhpur Tele No 591

OUR DIWALI & REPUBLIC-DAY ISSUES

OUTSTANDING MERITS OF OUR SPECIAL NUMBERS

FORWARD TIMES

SUBSCRIPTION RATES

Quarterly
Halfyearly
Annual

Editor FORWARD TIMES

Olympic Cinema Building

Editor: D. P. BHARGAVA

Jodhpur, Saturday the 16th. Feb. 1963.

2nd year
Special Issue 10 nP

RAJASTHAN PAYS TEARFUL HOMAGE TO SHAHEED SHAITAN SINGH

(From Forward Times News Service)

JODHPUR, Feb. 16.

Jodhpur—accords a befitting homage to Chushul Hero Major Shaitansingh of Banasar the recipient of Param Vir Chakra by President of India for most conspicuous bravery in the operations against the Chinese, whose dead body is to arrive here today by a special dakota. The body was handed over on Wednesday by the Chinese authorities. All the Rajasthan Ministers, Presidents Military Secretary, GOC Delhi area General B. S. Shekhawat and many high dignatories are expected to arrive here to participate in the funeral procession with full Military honours. The body is coming directly from Leh in Ladakh to Jodhpur by plane. The funeral procession will start from Air Force at 1 P.M. It will be recalled that only recently his wife received cash award of Rs. 30,000/- from the Chief Minister besides land and the Rajdadi Saheba, the Rajmata of Jodhpur and His Highness Jaipur had given each rupees one thousand one besides Hathi Sarupao. Major Shaitansingh died like historic Rajasthani heros. He was commanding an Infantry Battalion deployed in Chushul sector at a height of seventeen thousand feet. On November 18, 1962 Chinese forces subjected the company position to heavy artillery, mortar and small arms and fire attacking it with overwhelming strength and in several successive waves. During the action Major dominated the scene of operations and moved at great personal risk from one platoon post to another sustaining the morale of his hard pressed troops. His men inflicted heavy casualties on the enemy. Though wounded severely he refused to be evacuated. His supreme courage leadership and examplery devotion to duty inspired his company to fight gallantly to the last man. Since then his home town Banasar 111 miles from here had become place of Pilgrimage.

MAJOR SHAITAN SINGH.

A Newspaper clipping

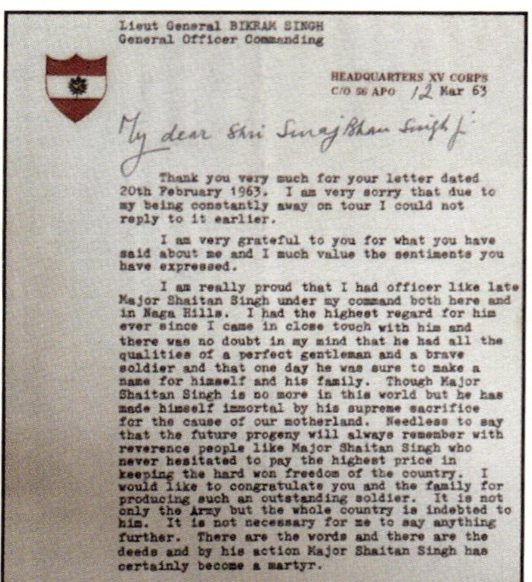

Lieut General BIKRAM SINGH
General Officer Commanding

HEADQUARTERS XV CORPS
C/O 56 APO 12 Mar 63

My dear Shri Suraj Bhan Singh ji

Thank you very much for your letter dated 20th February 1963. I am very sorry that due to my being constantly away on tour I could not reply to it earlier.

I am very grateful to you for what you have said about me and I much value the sentiments you have expressed.

I am really proud that I had officer like late Major Shaitan Singh under my command both here and in Naga Hills. I had the highest regard for him ever since I came in close touch with him and there was no doubt in my mind that he had all the qualities of a perfect gentleman and a brave soldier and that one day he was sure to make a name for himself and his family. Though Major Shaitan Singh is no more in this world but he has made himself immortal by his supreme sacrifice for the cause of our motherland. Needless to say that the future progeny will always remember with reverence people like Major Shaitan Singh who never hesitated to pay the highest price in keeping the hard won freedom of the country. I would like to congratulate you and the family for producing such an outstanding soldier. It is not only the Army but the whole country is indebted to him. It is not necessary for me to say anything further. There are the words and there are the deeds and by his action Major Shaitan Singh has certainly become a martyr.

pto

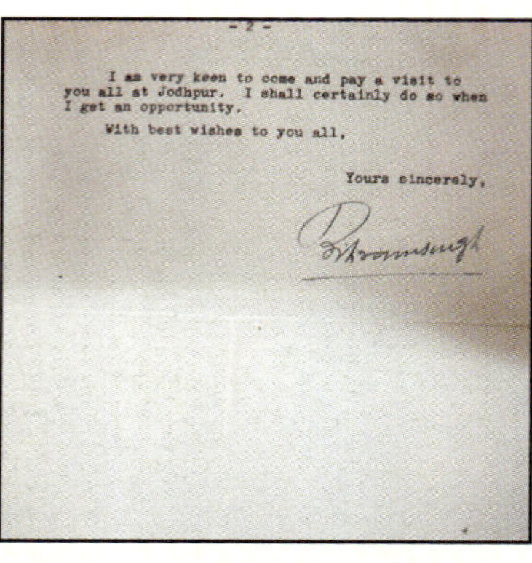

- 2 -

I am very keen to come and pay a visit to you all at Jodhpur. I shall certainly do so when I get an opportunity.

With best wishes to you all.

Yours sincerely,

Bikram Singh

Letter of Lt Gen Bikram Singh

Citation in respect of Major SHAITAN SINGH (IC-6400)
Kumaon Regiment (Posthumous)

...

Major Shaitan Singh was commanding a Company of an Infantry Battalion deployed at Rezangala in the Chushul Sector at a height of about 17,000 feet. The locality was isolated from the main defended Sector and consisted of 5 defended platoon positions. On 18th November 1962, the Chinese forces subjected the Company position to heavy artillery, mortar and small arms fire and attacked in overwhelming strength and in several successive waves. Against heavy odds, our troops beat back successive waves of enemy attack. During the action, Major Shaitan Singh dominated the scene of operations and moved at great personal risk from one platoon post to another sustaining the morale of his hard pressed platoon posts. While doing so he was seriously wounded but continued to encourage and lead his men who, following his brave example, fought gallantly and inflicted heavy casualties on the enemy. For every man lost by us, the enemy lost 4 or 5. When Major Shaitan Singh fell disabled by wounds in his arms and abdomen, his men tried to evacuate him, but came under heavy machine gun fire. Major Shaitan Singh then ordered his men to leave him to his fate in order to save their lives.

Major Shaitan Singh's supreme courage, leadership and exemplary devotion to duty inspired his Company to fight gallantly almost to the last man.

(P.V.R. RAO)
Secretary to the Government of India.

PVC Citation of Maj Shaitan Singh

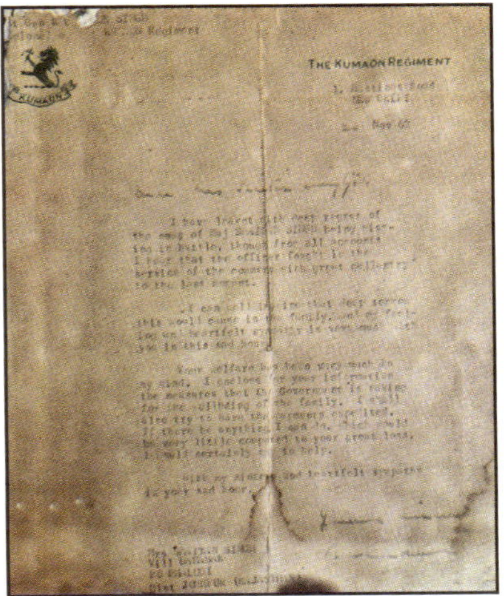

THE KUMAON REGIMENT

Letter of Lt Gen K Bahadur Singh

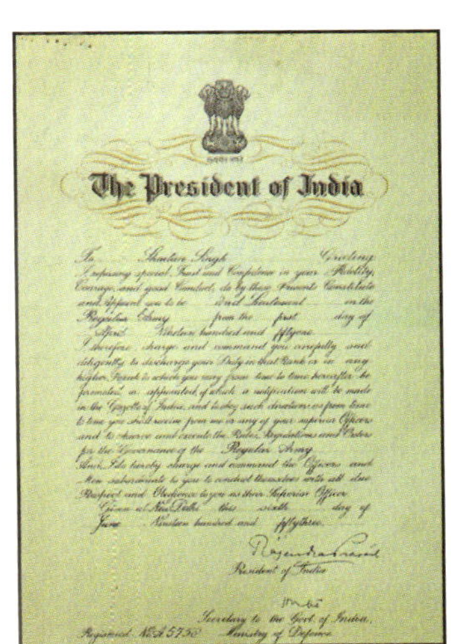

The President of India

Short Service Commission of 2/Lt Shaitan Singh

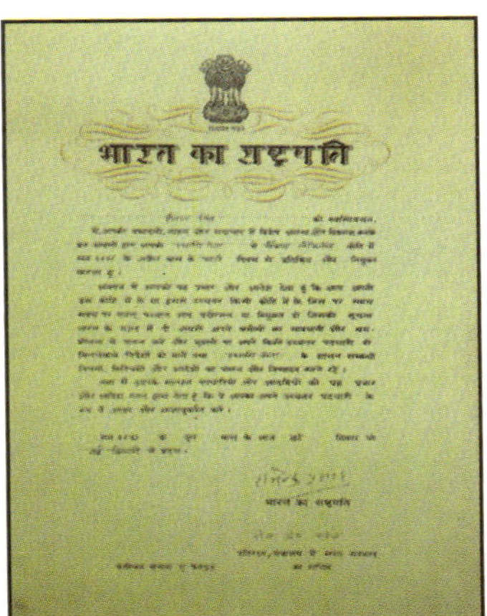

भारत का राष्ट्रपति

Short Service Commission of 2/Lt Shaitan Singh (Hindi)

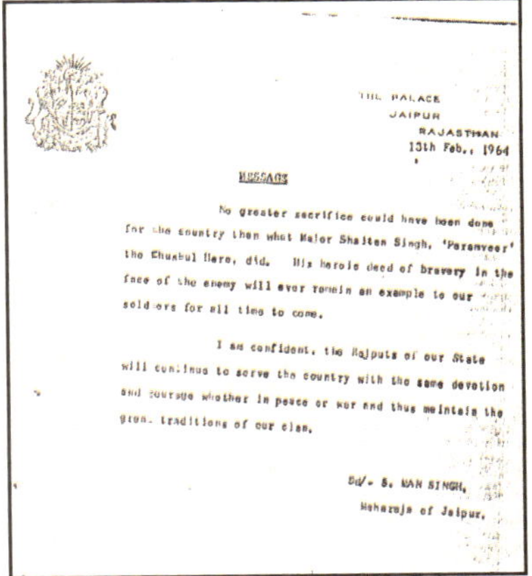

THE PALACE
JAIPUR
RAJASTHAN
13th Feb., 1964

MESSAGE

No greater sacrifice could have been done for the country than what Major Shaitan Singh, 'Paramveer' the Chushul Hero, did. His heroic deed of bravery in the face of the enemy will ever remain an example to our soldiers for all time to come.

I am confident, the Rajputs of our State will continue to serve the country with the same devotion and courage whether in peace or war and thus maintain the great traditions of our clan.

Sd/- S. MAN SINGH,
Maharaja of Jaipur.

Letter from Brig Sawai Man Singh, MVC of Jaipur

Shoulder Pips of Lt Shaitan Singh

Capt Shaitan Singh (standing in the middle) during a field exercise

Capt Shaitan Singh with some officials

Lt Shaitan Singh with his friends

Capt Shaitan Singh posing on the bank of a river

Capt Shaitan Singh (sitting in the middle) during a field exercise

Wrist watch of Maj Shaitan Singh retrieved from his mortal remains

23 Infantry Division shoulder patch of Capt Shaitan Singh

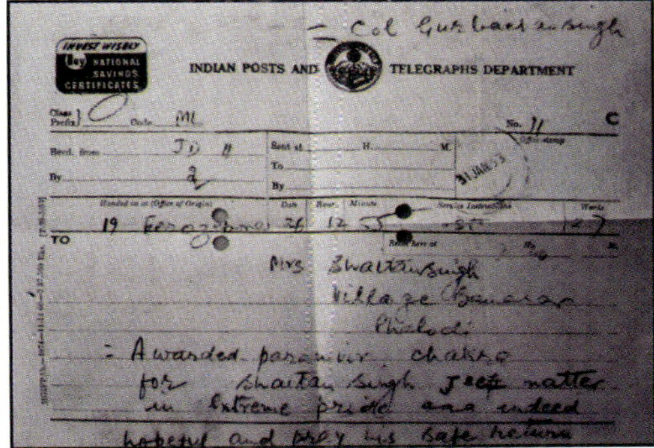

Col Gurbachan Singh

INVEST WISELY NATIONAL SAVINGS CERTIFICATES

INDIAN POSTS AND TELEGRAPHS DEPARTMENT

Mrs Shaitan Singh
Village Banasar
Phalodi

Awarded paramvir chakra for Shaitan Singh ... in extreme pride and indeed hopeful and pray his safe return

A telegram with news of Maj Shaitan Singh being conferred PVC

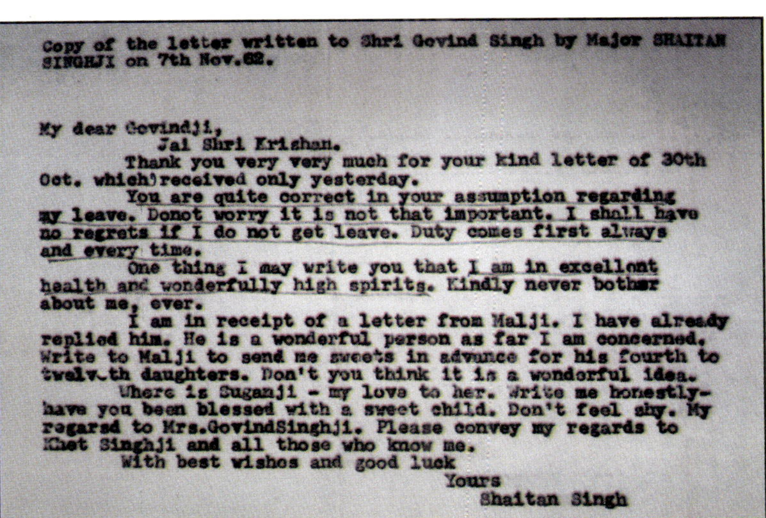

Copy of the letter written to Shri Govind Singh by Major SHAITAN SINGHJI on 7th Nov.62.

My dear Govindji,
Jai Shri Krishan.

Thank you very very much for your kind letter of 30th Oct. which)received only yesterday.

You are quite correct in your assumption regarding my leave. Donot worry it is not that important. I shall have no regrets if I do not get leave. Duty comes first always and every time.

One thing I may write you that I am in excellent health and wonderfully high spirits. Kindly never bother about me, ever.

I am in receipt of a letter from Malji. I have already replied him. He is a wonderful person as far I am concerned. Write to Malji to send me sweets in advance for his fourth to twelv.th daughters. Don't you think it is a wonderful idea.

Where is Suganji - my love to her. Write me honestly- have you been blessed with a sweet child. Don't feel shy. My regared to Mrs.GovindSinghji. Please convey my regards to Khet Singhji and all those who know me.

With best wishes and good luck

Yours
Shaitan Singh

A letter of Maj Shaitan Singh from the War front

Temple of Maj Shaitan Singh, PVC in his village

Native house of Maj Shaitan Singh, PVC

Maj Shaitan Singh in traditional clothes during a family function

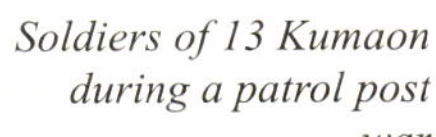

Soldiers of 13 Kumaon during a patrol post war

Gen KS Thimayya meeting officers of 13 Kumaon, Ambala

A wall of Rezang La Memorial dedicated to Maj Shaitan Singh, PVC

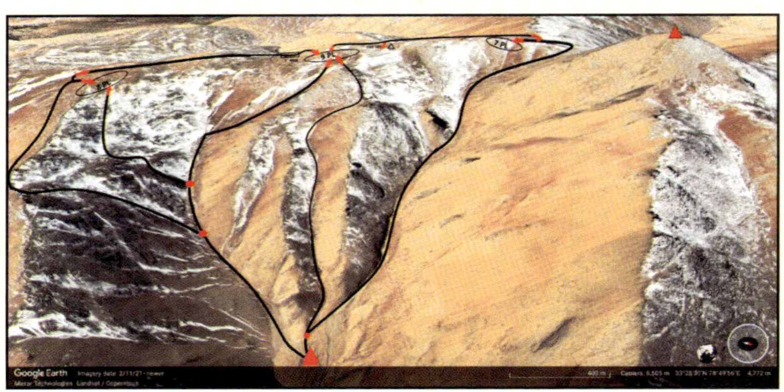

Map of Rezang La attacks

Map of Chushul

camp of the Ahang (rebel governor), on May 17, being the most important during this period. Ahang escaped minus his right foot. However, his entourage were not that fortunate.

The 14 Rajput joined the division's fighting squad. In July, Shaitan appeared for the Part C exam, and later he appeared for Part D exam which used to be promotional exams for captain-rank officers to be eligible for promotion to the rank of major. Shaitan passed both the exams and became eligible for the rank of major.

An Evacuation

A company of 14 Rajput under the command of Maj Piara Singh was stationed at Jotsoma, a short distance from the divisional headquarters. During an operation, the company suffered a casualty at its post. Shaitan was assigned the charge of managing the evacuation effort in the insurgent-controlled area. He was instructed to dispatch an unaccompanied ambulance to the post to bring the casualty. Additionally, he was tasked to gather information on the situation if the attack on the post was significant. After a considerable period, the evacuation was successfully completed with the aid of Piara Singh and locals, who gave the ambulance cover.

The Lotha Naga tribe of the Wokha area were better behaved than the Sema (or Sümi) Naga tribe in the Lumami area. The insurgents frequently engaged the patrols that 13 Kumaon sent out into the new region. Throughout the months of May, June, and July of 1959, they successfully retrieved a sizable number of weapons from the communities. A new operation against the insurgents, codenamed "Operation Wodehouse", was to be planned along the lines of Operation Jhoom. It was to be launched in August. However, by then, the insurgents had relocated elsewhere because of the battalion's robust and aggressive patrolling in their area. As a result, Operation Wodehouse didn't yield particularly spectacular results, except for the elimination of a notorious "brigadier" of the NHG, who had unleashed a reign of terror in the area for some time.

23rd Infantry Division

On September 1, 1959, a major change occurred in the division. The GOC Assam was redesignated as GOC 23 Infantry Division. The division was originally raised on January 1, 1942, at Jhansi in central India to participate in the Second World War. The division was re-raised by the Indian Army on September 1, 1959, for the Nagaland insurgency when GOC Assam was redesignated as GOC 23rd Infantry Division. Maj Gen Bikram Singh, who as 181 Independent Brigade Group commander had already served in the area, was chosen to command the division during the peak of the Naga insurgency. However, the redesignation of the division did not hamper the operations. They were carried out as usual with the same vigour.

For the 13 Kumaon, the final four months of 1959 were quiet. But three operations happened quickly one after the other in the new year, 1960. Among them, "Operation Madhu" (January-February 1960) was a major counter-insurgency campaign. The two other operations – "Operation Siano" and "Operation Golmal" were minor counter-insurgency campaigns that were launched in quick succession that year.

Bikram, the Tiger and His Staff Captain

Brig Raghunath V. Jatar, who became a close friend of Major Shaitan Singh, remembers an incident that the major himself told him on a few occasions.

Jatar recalls: "In the late 1950s, Major Shaitan Singh was a captain on the staff of the 23 Infantry Division, which was headed by Bikram Singh, who was a Major General at that time. Maj Gen Bikram was a down-to-earth soldier who was very tough on anyone who didn't put his weight on assigned duties. In fact, he was a 'terror' for his men. However, he understood Shaitan, who was a captain then, and was very fond of him."

"Once, Bikram Singh was out on a tour of an Assam Rifles unit that was under his jurisdiction. They reached their destination in the evening and settled for the night in two rooms. Shaitan was allotted a type of room normally given to captains. Shaitan, being a simple man, was satisfied with the allocated room and had no complaints. Next morning during breakfast, Bikram Singh asked him where he stayed for the night. The captain told him the truth about the room. Just then, the Assam Rifles unit's commanding officer, a lieutenant colonel, for senior to Captain Shaitan Singh, walked in. Before the colonel could settle in his chair, Gen Bikram started shouting at him and said, 'What did he mean by assigning an ordinary room to his staff captain? Shaitan felt extremely embarrassed that the colonel got a dressing down because of him. How could he say that (about the room) to 'Tiger' Bikram? he thought."

As luck would have it, Bikram Singh rose to become a lieutenant general and was a corps commander at Udhampur in 1962. He had the unique pleasure of recommending Maj Shaitan Singh for a well-deserved Param Vir Chakra for his valour in the war with China.

Bikram Singh and Shaitan had a special fraternal relationship. He had spent plenty of time working with him. Shaitan was always regarded as the general's younger brother.

Time to Say Goodbye

The winter of 1960 started to thaw, and Shaitan went for his annual leave of two months. His leave was about to end in the first week of April. When he came back, his unit was preparing to move, and time had finally come for the 13 Kumaon to bid the Nagas farewell after a long campaign of counter-insurgency operations, on April 24, 1960. However, Shaitan still had six months left to complete his tenure as GSO-3 in the 48 Infantry Brigade, under which the 13 Kumaon was attached.

During his time at the division, Shaitan made some good friends with his colleagues. Capt Magni Ram (who later went on to command 15 Dogra) was one of them. Lt Col DS Sidhu, the GSO-1 of the divisional headquarters, was another. Also, by this time, the insurgency had taken a reverse turn. The frequency of operations had significantly reduced. In October, both Shaitan Singh and Magni Ram received the movement order to move to their respective units as their tenure in the division had come to an end.

For the first time in six years after being transferred to 13 Kumaon, Shaitan was going to serve with the unit as its own officer.

On November 4, Shaitan and Magni Ram left Kohima for the Manipur Road from where they had to go on their own ways. The friends departed never to meet again. Shaitan went to Ambala, which he reached on November 7 to join his parent unit for the first time.

Capt Shaitan Singh received the General Service Medal for his notable and exceptional service in the Naga Hills. It was his first medal in his military service.

References

1. Interview with Mr Narpat Singh s/o Maj Shaitan Singh, PVC
2. Interview with Mr Mahendra Singh Nephew of Maj Shaitan Singh, PVC
3. Letters of Major Shaitan Singh
4. Interview with Brigadier Raghunath V Jatar (retd)
5. Interview with Mrs Anand Kanwar d/o Lt Col Bijai Singh
6. Documents of Major Shaitan Singh, PVC
7. Telephonic Interview with Mr Sandeep Kang Grandson of Lt Gen Bikram Singh

❑

Major Shaitan Singh

Terah Kumaon

Captain Shaitan Singh, 13 Kumaon

This chapter focuses on the tenure of Maj Shaitan Singh with 13 Kumaon at Ambala. This was his first tenure with his parent unit. This chapter talks of his time as 3-inch mortar platoon commander. It takes us to the details of Operation Vijay and the visits of two colonels of the regiment. The chapter includes Maj Shaitan Singh's last leave at home and the weddings of his juniors.

On the Gates of 13

On November 7, 1960, Shaitan arrived in Ambala. He checked in at 13 Kumaon's unit location. Shaitan had been transferred to 13 Kumaon in 1954, but till this point, it was only on paper. Although he had occasionally visited the unit in Naga Hills, this was the first time in six years that he was going to serve within the unit. The 48 Infantry Brigade and the 17 Infantry Division, both of which were based at Ambala, were in command of the unit.

The Kumaon Regiment's 13th Battalion holds the distinction of being the first raised in the regiment after Independence. On August 5, 1948, the unit at Kanpur started to take shape under Lt Col H.C. Taylor, with an equal number of Kumaonis and Ahirs. The regiment was prepared to join the 202 Infantry Brigade at Barrackpore on July 1, 1949, and assume its place alongside other infantry battalions of the Indian Army. It changed location to Fort William (Calcutta) a few months later. Prior to arriving in Ambala, the battalion had served in Kashmir and Nagaland. The unit saw a significant change in its class composition during the time it was deployed in Naga Hills.

Given the small number of Ahirs in the battalions, there was a promotion limitation for them. As a result, the Indian Army Headquarters decided in January 1959 that 13 Kumaon should be transformed into a 100 percent Ahir Battalion. This would be accomplished by moving its Kumaonis to the 2nd and 6th Battalions and sending their Ahirs to the 13th, making the 2nd and 6th Battalion all-Kumaoni in the process.

A decision was made at the battalion commanders' conference, which was held in May 1959, that the change-over should be completed in two phases: the interchange between the 13 Kumaon and the 2 Kumaon was to be carried out in small batches and completed by the end of the year. The interchange between the 13 Kumaon and the 6 Kumaon was decided to be spread over the first five months of 1960.

The transition went off smoothly without a hitch while the 13 Kumaon was occupied with operational duties in the Naga Hills, which is noteworthy.

When Shaitan arrived at the "Gate of the 13th", he was led to 129 Allen By Lines – the officers' mess of the 13 Kumaon. Shaitan was given access to a room reserved for single officers. Throughout his whole career, Shaitan never travelled with his family, not even for a vacation or to any of his postings.

Later that day, after Shaitan had settled into his room, he ran across four subalterns – all bachelors from the 13 Kumaon who lived in the mess. They were Lt D.D. Saklani, Lt B.S. Lamba, Lt R.K. Khanna and 2/Lt Prem Kumar.

Shaitan joined the office of the unit a few days later, and on November 22, as the only captain to have completed the 3-inch mortar course, he was chosen to lead the battalion's 3-inch mortar platoon. His dining-in party was that same evening.

Dined-In

On November 22, Shaitan received an invitation to the officers' mess, where the 13 Kumaon officers had arranged a dine-in party. The commanding officer of the 13th, Lt Col Bhupal Singh Chand, VrC, who took over command of the unit just two months ago, joined the celebration. Col Chand was a part of the 3 Kumaon Rifles and took part in the Jammu & Kashmir operations in 1947-48 as the company commander, for which he was awarded the Vir Chakra. Maj Sukhdarshan Singh, the second in command; Maj J.N. Kunzru, Major Girish Narayan Sinha, Maj Gadigeppa Halgali, an officer who served with the 13 Kumaon since its raising at Kanpur; Maj H.N. Sur, Capt H.S. Chauhan, Capt Raghunath Jatar, Lt D.D. Saklani, Lt B.S. Lamba, Lt RK Khanna, and 2/Lt Prem Kumar, 2/Lt P.M. Wakhle were also present. Given that Shaitan had previously interacted with each of them in the Naga Hills and that they were all aware of his abstinence from alcohol, he was not offered a drink. As the celebration was coming to an end, the CO came up to Shaitan and welcomed him to the unit. "You will make the paltan proud, I'm quite sure of it," the CO said. Thereafter, Shaitan was asked to sign the mess's visitors' book.

The following day, the battalion's regular activities began. Shaitan went on to command the 3-inch mortar unit for a while.

Brig Raghunath Jatar, remembering an incident from 1960, says: "We were at the battalion officers' mess in Ambala in 1960, enjoying an evening party. Shaitan Singh, being shy, was in a corner along with one male colleague and me. We were having innocent fun and laughing quite a lot. After a while, I moved on, and Mrs Kunzru, the wife of a senior major, J.N. Kunzru, complimented me. When I asked what the compliments were for, she said, 'You made Capt Shaitan Singh laugh so much!' Shaitan, who was a captain then, was a pleasant character but quiet and reserved by nature and rather shy with ladies. He was so quiet that he rarely laughed."

Jatar recalls another incident and says that while their unit was stationed in Ambala, the CO, Lt Col B.S. Chand, asked Shaitan to play football for the battalion team, knowing that Shaitan was a former national-level footballer. But then, Shaitan was out of touch with the game and had severe pain in the knee. However, he was most embarrassed to admit that to the CO. Jatar says he doesn't remember if Shaitan played for the team or not, but he couldn't say "no" to the CO.

In April 1961, the-then Army chief and the colonel of the Kumaon Regiment, Gen K.S. Thimmaiya, was scheduled to vacate his position on May 8. He was supposed to visit 13 Kumaon at Ambala. The unit had undergone a few changes prior to this.

The battalion also included Maj Mukut Singh and Maj Jaswant Singh, who was a senior subaltern with Shaitan in 6 Kumaon. Maj Gulab Singh had left. Maj Kunzru was now assigned to a United Nations force. The general's visit was the primary focus of the unit and intense preparations were carried out.

After finishing his assignment with a UN force in Laos, Maj H.S. Dhingra rejoined the unit and assumed the position of second in command as Maj Sukhdarshan Singh had left the unit. His family was scheduled to arrive in a few days. To live with her spouse, Mrs Dhingra travelled to Ambala with her daughter and two boys. The following day, while Maj Dhingra was taking his son, Haramrit, to the mess, Haramrit noticed a man standing in the shadows inside the mess window. Out of curiosity, he asked his father, "Who is he?"

Replying to his boy's curious query, the major said, "The man in half light is Capt Shaitan Singh." Haramrit's initial impression of Maj Shaitan Singh was this, which stayed with him all his life. Later, Haramrit served in the Regiment of the Artillery for twenty years. However, he is prouder to call himself a Kumaoni than a gunner. Today, he speaks admiringly of Shaitan Singh.

Haramrit's sister, Mrs Sunita Mukherjee, recalls: "When we arrived in Ambala, we met Capt Shaitan Singh, who was a very quiet but kind man. During the days we spent in the unit, he hardly ever spoke. She also recalls that he provided swimming lessons in the unit's pool to all the officers' children.

Lt Gen Ramesh Hagali, son of Maj G. Hagali, who has served in the unit since its formation, recalls Shaitan Singh as a very kind person who treated everyone with respect. The unit's youngsters and children admired him.

The General and Shaitan

April was coming to an end. The Army chief Gen K.S. Thimmaiya paid a two-day visit to the unit. Lt Col S.Y. Munshi, the general's military adviser, accompanied the chief. Following a ceremonial introduction with the officers, the general received a guard of honour. A group photograph of officers and ladies with the general was taken.

Thimmaiya attended a reception as its chief guest, which was hosted at the officers' mess that same evening. The unit's CO led the general into the party where he was greeted by all the officers and ladies. The celebration eventually included all the officers serving with the unit at that time. The subalterns listened to the general as he spoke to them, while holding their drinks in their hands. The general then noticed a calm man standing with his drinking companions, but was empty-handed. The general headed in his direction and the CO followed him.

Thimmaiya reached Shaitan, shook hands with him and asked: "What is your name, son?"

Shaitan, in a gentle voice, replied: "Sir, I'm Captain Shaitan Singh."

Thimmaiya: "Gentleman, why aren't you having a drink?"

Then, the general offered Shaitan a drink, to which Shaitan replied: "Sir, I don't drink. I'm a teetotaller."

Thimmaiya: "Is it?!" Then laughing, the general jokingly said: "Fir toh tumhara naam Shaitan nahi, Shareef hona chahiye. (Then your name shouldn't be Shaitan, it should be Shareef.)"

Shaitan was a teetotaller. He never drank alcohol and refused it on many such occasions, including in his dining-in parties.

Sports competitions were held the following day, and the Charlie Company, which was commanded by the second in command, Maj H.S. Dhingra, won. The winning team's photo with Gen Thimmaiya was displayed after the competition.

On the same day, the unit bade farewell to the general. On May 8, 1961, Thimmaiya retired from the Army after serving for four years as its chief of staff. He also handed over the baton of the colonel of the regiment on that date, although he remained the honorary colonel of the Kumaon Regiment.

The Last Leave

The battalion resumed its usual duties and exercises. It was summer, a time of year when large parts of the country experience intense heat. Shaitan used to live alone, therefore he frequently received invitations to friends' homes for lunch or dinner. He made plans for his annual leave and wrote a letter to his brother, Surajbhan Singh, stating that he needed a house to rent in Jodhpur again. Midway through May, he applied for his annual leave, which was approved for two months but only began in the following month, June. Shaitan reached Jodhpur on June 6. Suraj had already arranged a house on rent for him in Jodhpur. He got the same bungalow where Shaitan lived two years ago. The following day, Shaitan's family arrived in Jodhpur, and this time his friends from 20 Rajput, Capt Mal Singh and Maj Rewat Singh were on leave. The two Rajput officers formerly resided on different floors of the same home.

Mrs Sagar Kanwar daughter of Col Rewat Singh recalls those times: "Col Mal Singh's family and my family shared a home. When Maj Shaitan Singh visited our house, all these friends would play cards for hours on end since they loved the game so much."

On this occasion, Shaitan played cards with his buddies for the final time, unaware that it was also his last leave ever.

Narpat couldn't travelled to stay with his father during his leave from Ajmer, where he attended school. Lal Singh, Shaitan's younger brother who was studying agriculture in Agra University, also met him at Jodhpur. Being very close to his brother-in-law, Mool Singh, Shaitan also spent a few days at his sister's house.

He remained in Jodhpur till the very last day of July before leaving on August 1 for Ambala without being aware that it was his final leave. His relatives forbade him from travelling that day since, according to traditional beliefs, it was a bad day. But Shaitan insisted.

He was never going to return to Jodhpur, where he had grown up and gone to high school, a city where he began his military career and gained notoriety as a footballer. He departed from Jodhpur unaware that he would never again see his mother, wife, brothers, sisters, and son.

On August 3, Shaitan travelled to Ambala and joined his duties there the next day. He was concerned about his family this time after returning from leave. He sent frequent letters to his son's hostel warden, Harish Chandra Mittal, inquiring about his health and academic progress. He wanted to see his son admitted to a biology course at a higher level and was anxious at this time because his wife's health was also not great.

He Got Posted to IMA

In the middle of November, Shaitan, the commander of the 3-inch mortar platoon for the 13 Kumaon Regiment, received an order instructing that he should report to the Indian Military Academy in Prem Nagar, Dehradun for a demonstration. Shaitan and his battalion began planning for the demonstration at the IMA. The detachment started moving for Dehradun. Shaitan's platoon was attached to the IMA once they arrived in Dehradun, where they had to demonstrate to the cadets how to operate a 3-inch mortar.

Operation Vijay

The situation in Goa was steadily deteriorating around that time. Some foreign enclaves continued to exist in India even after Independence. These included Goa, Daman, and Diu under Portugal and Pondicherry, Chandernagore, Yaman, and Mahe under France. Following negotiations, the French decided to give those territories up to India. The Portuguese, on the other hand, adopted a more rigid stance.

The Goans staged satyagraha and mass civil disobedience to overthrow the colonisers and join India, but the Portuguese brutally suppressed them. Their anti-India foreign policy also grew increasingly strong. According to reports from 1961, they were discussing with Pakistan to build a joint military base in Goa.

November 1961 marked the terrible and aminous turn of the situation. An officer was wounded on November 18 when Portuguese soldiers stationed on Anjidiv Island opened fire on an Indian passenger ship. A few days later, shots were fired at an Indian fishing boat. The movement of Pakistani forces on India's western borders was also reported at the same time. Owing to these factors, the government decided to launch "Operation Vijay'' to liberate Goa. The situation called for swift action and forced the government's hand.

All the 13 Kumaon officers and detachments had their temporary assignments stopped and they were summoned back. The battalion reunited with Shaitan and his demonstration squad after they reached Ambala. Capt Balbir Singh Lamba, a Kumaoni officer who was set to wed Ms Sheela, the daughter of Col Padam Singh, the first Indian to command 4 Kumaon and the commandant of the Kumaon Regimental Centre, when he got his orders to return to the unit.

The wedding was scheduled for December 4, but the 13 Kumaon, as a unit of the 48 Infantry Brigade under Brig Gurbax Singh's command, had to head from Ambala to Belgaum on December 5. Capt Lamba's two-month-long wedding-related leave was reduced to three days.

Therefore, Capt Lamba also travelled to Belgaum to join the unit just three days after the wedding. Under the direction of Maj

Gen Kunhiraman Palat Candeth, the entire 17 Infantry Division had moved. The divisional force mainly consisted of 2 Sikh Light Infantry, 2 Bihar, 3 Sikh, 4 Sikh, 4 Rajput, 2 Grenadiers and 13 Kumaon with 7 Mahar (MMG).

There were reportedly 4,500 Portuguese soldiers in Goa. Operation Vijay was planned as a two-pronged assault: the 50 Independent Para Brigade and 17 Infantry Division (48 and 63 Infantry Brigades) were to attack from the north on the Dodamarg-Assonora-Bicholim and the Anmod-Molem-Ponda axis, respectively. A battalion group from each was to launch simultaneous assaults on Daman and Diu. The Indian Air Force was to provide tactical assistance to the ground forces while destroying the airfields and radio station in Goa. The Indian Navy was to seize Anjidiv Island and blockade Goa. December 18 was D-day. The division deployed 2 SikhLI, 2 Bihar, 3 Sikh, 4 Sikh, and 4 Rajput, but 13 Kumaon was held up.

As intended, the Indian troops breached the Goa frontline. The 50 Para Brigade, led by Brig Sagat Singh, made quicker progress from the north, and by the early hours of December 19, Panjim, the capital city, had fallen. The 112 Brigade was engaged in fighting the Portuguese in Diu. The Portuguese did not put up a strong fight in Goa, but their garrisons in Daman and Diu fought valiantly till they finally gave up.

The operations in Daman and Diu were managed by 20 Rajput and 1 Maratha. The 20 Rajput's companies arrived at the creek to launch their assault. Some of the Rajput boats capsized because of Portuguese MMG and LMG fire in Diu. Maj Mal Singh, Shaitan's close friend, advanced and crossed the creek with five more men. He and his soldiers attacked the LMG trenches at Fort-de-Cova after they arrived at the far bank and silenced them. Mal Singh and two of his soldiers were injured by Portuguese MMG fire that came from a different location. Mal Singh's right arm was severely wounded. However, the three injured were bravely brought to shore by the company's havildar major, Mohan Singh, and two other soldiers.

The battalion took 403 Portuguese prisoners of war. The lieutenant governor of Diu surrendered, which Brig Jaswant Singh, commander of the 112 Infantry Brigade, accepted.

After four and a half centuries of foreign domination, the Portuguese soldiers at Goa, Daman, and Diu, led by the colonial governor general, Manuel António Vassalo e Silva, surrendered.

Although Operation Vijay was over in less than 36 hours, the Portuguese troops' weapons and ammunition had to be obtained and booby traps had to be removed – first at Ponda, then at Panjim and Velha Goa. These tasks fell to the troops of 13 Kumaon, who had seen no combat.

Through a letter from Lt Malhotra of the 20 Rajput, Shaitan learned of the wounds sustained by Mal Singh in January. Mal Singh, who was initially treated in Jamnagar and later transferred to the Military Hospital in Poona, received an anxious letter from Shaitan.

The letter, dated January 9, 1962, reads:

"My dearest brother, Jaishri Krishan. It gave me a very severe shock but later immense pleasure to learn from Lt Malhotra that, although you were severely wounded, you stood most magnificently, for which you have been recommended for an award. Now that you are out of danger, I congratulate you from the core of my heart for Rajput on the battlefield.

Mal ji I assure you, you are very lucky to get an opportunity to fight, whereas I did absolutely nothing here."

This letter shows that Shaitan wanted to fight for his unit and country, but his unit did not get the chance to engage in actual combat.

The unit was occupied with guarding the Portuguese prisoners in the camp and making sure that their possessions weren't taken or robbed. Shaitan had an accident during this time, which resulted in injuries to his right hand. He was unable to write due to the severity of his injury, which prevented him from writing letters to his loved ones.

In the Memories

The battalion was travelling to Ambala when it found itself in Mumbai during the third week of February 1962.

Brigadier Raghunath Jatar describes an event that took place in Mumbai as: "I recall once informing Major Shaitan that I had probably killed a street puppy dog when I ran over it on a motorbike. He closed his eyes and prayed silently, and I knew he was hurt. Just goes to show how kind he was."

The battalion could not return to Ambala till February 18. Capt R.K. Khanna only had a brief stay in Ambala before receiving approval for two months of leave for his wedding. On March 1, Khanna got married. Officers of the 13 Kumaon attended his wedding. A short time later, in March, the battalion was dispatched on a training exercise, and Capt DD Saklani was assigned for a temporary staff posting in the 50 Para Brigade in Kashmir. The battalion was kept busy by the frequent exercise camps that were held one after another. Capt ED Wayte, who was posted with the 14 Jammu & Kashmir Militia, had rejoined the unit.

Lt Gen Kanwar Bahadur Singh was scheduled to pay the unit a visit in March. He was from a royal family in Palaitha, Kota, and was originally from 4 Kumaon. He joined the 4 Kumaon in October 1932. He had led the 5th and 4th Infantry Divisions. In October 1959, after serving for three years as adjutant general, he was named commandant of the National Defence College. On May 8, 1961, he was appointed colonel of the Kumaon Regiment. During his visit, Capt Shaitan Singh was designated as his escort.

Brig Prem Kumar, a subaltern in 13 Kumaon, recalls his superior and fraternal figure, Maj Shaitan Singh, saying that he lived in the officers' mess with the unit's bachelor officers.

Prem Kumar recalls: "He was older than all of us. Sometimes, if a junior turned up late for lunch or supper, he would wait for him before beginning his meal. He never argued with anyone or demanded to know why he was late. He joined us for every supper and never spoke to us as his juniors. Rather, he always regarded us like younger brothers."

"In 1962, my marriage to Shobha was arranged by a mutual acquaintance. We were scheduled to get married on April 16. Maj Shaitan Singh was overjoyed for me. He and Saklani were present during my Pathankot wedding. Even throughout the reception, Maj Shaitan looked so elegant while donning a turban. Since my mother appreciated him so much, she prepared dinner for them and served them personally as it got close to their departure for Ambala."

Shaitan Singh and Saklani boarded a train for Ambala on their way back from Pathankot. On the train, they ran into a palm reader. Out of curiosity they requested the palmist to predict their future. The palmist read the lines on Shaitan's palm. In Saklani's presence, the palmist told Shaitan that something extraordinary was soon going to happen in his life which would make him famous.

Maj Shaitan Singh's valiant death in the battlefield, as recalled by Brig Raghunath Jatar, proved the prophecy of the palmist correct.

Mrs Sheela Lamba, the wife of Brig Balbir Singh Lamba, who was a senior subaltern when Capt Shaitan joined 13 Kumaon, recalls: "My husband was quite fond of him (Shaitan) and that he was like a brother to him. He used to come over for lunch or dinner when we were in Ambala." She also remembered Shaitan as a very gentle and kind person.

May 1962 finally arrived. Capt Khanna by now brought his family back into the unit. His wife, Mrs Rani Khanna, recollects that after the evening games, Capt Shaitan Singh, Capt Saklani, Lt Prem Kumar, and Capt Lamba visited their home for tea and coffee. They all lived together. She recounts: "My mother-in-law used to be there with us, and she was fond of Maj Shaitan Singh. She invited him for lunch or dinner as he used to stay alone." Mrs Khanna also remembers Shaitan as a very "gentle" and "modest" individual.

The unit had received the orders to depart for Baramulla in Kashmir the next month. Before handing over the reins on May 6, Lt Col B.S. Chand had dispatched an advance party to Baramulla. As 13 Kumaon's sixth commanding officer, Lt Col Hari Singh Dhingra assumed command, elevating Maj Girish Narayan Sinha to the position of second in command and Capt Shaitan Singh to that of Charlie Company commander. Capt H.N. Sur and Maj G. Hagali had left the battalion to perform extra regimental duties, and the battalion had begun preparing for the relocation.

Baramulla

The main body of the unit began moving to Baramulla for its field assignment the following month. The entire force consolidated at Baramulla on June 14 under the command of Brig ETC Sen led the 268th Infantry Brigade of the 19th Infantry Division. In the brigade, 13 Kumaon had joined 3 Para (Kumaon) and 1 Jat Light Infantry. Shaitan had previously served under the division between the years of 1949 and 1950 while assigned to the Kotah Umed Infantry in Dras.

The battalion had 16 officers when it arrived in Baramulla a few days earlier, but after some time some of them were posted elsewhere, including Capt R.K. Khanna who was moved to the Srinagar subarea and Capt R.V. Jatar who went on leave to prepare for his impending course at staff college.

Shaitan, who had been designated as the 13 Kumaon's quartermaster, performed additional responsibilities with the other officers. The division's 5 Jat unit was transferred from Uri to Ladakh at this same moment to relieve the 1/8 Gorkha Rifles.

In addition to 1 Jat (LI), 3 Para (Kumaon), 13 Field Regiment, and 63rd Cavalry, the 13 Kumaon was now participating in a collective training exercise. The Ahirs scaled higher altitudes during their training. After the troops had settled in following their training in September, Shaitan requested his annual leave a few days later. He was assured by the CO that he would get his annual leave.

On the evening of September 14, the higher-ups sent a message instructing Lt Col H.S. Dhingra, who was in the hospital because of his poor health, to prepate the battalion for the transfer to Leh. The news of Paltan's relocation quickly swept through the ranks the next day. Since no one knew why they were relocating to Leh, the atmosphere in the unit was tense.

Maj Girish Narayan Sinha, the officiating CO in charge, asked each officer to instruct their respective companies on how to get ready for the move.

Dhingra insisted on moving with the unit despite the doctors' reluctance to allow him to do so. To obtain an authorisation of leave from the hospital, he even had to sign a risk certificate. Maj Jaswant Singh was also refused to move with the unit to high altitude due to his medical category. Around September 18, the unit was supposed to leave from Baramulla. Instead of moving the entire battalion at once, the orders called for moving one company at a time.

The officers and JCOs were assigned several tasks to do to get the battalion ready to move. As the officer in charge of the rear party, Maj Shaitan Singh transferred temporary control of the Charlie Company to Lt Prem Kumar, the company officer. The CO informed Shaitan that when the entire battalion arrives at the new location his leave would be sanctioned.

The first convoy was sent to Srinagar on September 18. All companies eventually found themselves travelling to Leh in a sequential pattern, with the final convoy departing on September 30 from Srinagar and Sonmarg, where they were required to spend the night and receive high-altitude and snow equipment. The following stop was in Kargil at Bodh Kharbu. The battalion reached Leh to join the 114th Infantry Brigade after a gruelling four-day trip. The current information the battalion had indicated that the battalion would relocate to Chushul in March of the following year.

Rear Party OC

Shaitan was now attached to 3 Para (Kumaon) and residing in the unit's mess while he was still at Baramulla to transfer duties and return the supplies.

Maj Shaitan Singh is remembered as a quiet and incredibly humble man by his former counterpart from 1 Jat (LI), Col S.P. Dua. He says: "Because we both served as the quartermaster for our separate units, we had many interactions. His unit was shifted to Ladakh earlier than our unit. I recall him remaining behind with the battalion rear.

On October 8, while Shaitan was preoccupied with his regular responsibilities, the Chinese began prodding the Indian forces stationed in forward positions. It was quite evident from then on that he was headed to the front, not home. He informed his friend Mal Singh about it and suspected that his leave may get cancelled.

On October 1, the 13 Kumaon's Bravo Company was instructed to relocate from the brigade headquarters in Leh. On the very next day, Shaitan received a message from the CO to quickly complete the tasks and join the unit at Leh.

Maj Mal Singh, in his letter to Maj Shaitan Singh dated October 14, 1962, writes:

"My dear Rakhu

How happy I am to receive a kind letter from you. I am glad that you are fine and in the best of spirits. I know why you are staying with the Para Regiment. I wish you the best of luck and success.

A soldier is fortunate to get the opportunity to serve the motherland in difficult times. I wish I was fit enough to avail myself of a similar opportunity again."

This letter was an unintentional reply to the letter written by Shaitan on January 9, 1962, in which he had stated: *"Mal ji I assure you, you are really lucky to get an opportunity to fight, whereas I did absolutely nothing here."*

Shaitan stayed with 3 Para (Kumaon) for a few days before taking the battalion rear to Srinagar, from where they had to move to Leh.

When Shaitan arrived in Srinagar, he started working on finishing his tasks right away. When the day was through, Capt R.K. Khanna met him and drove him to his house since his mother had called Shaitan over for lunch and prepared some delectable dishes, like Kumaoni raita.

While having lunch, Shaitan talked about the CO's reprimand to him, in which the CO had said: "You are delaying the move and coming over to Ladakh."

Since Shaitan had so much work to do and focused on his duties, the CO's unfavourable words hurt him. He appeared disheartened and had tears in his eyes as he spoke about it, recalls Mrs Rani Khanna. She adds that he had requested for his annual leave but that it was being delayed.

Mrs Khanna says: "My mother-in-law, who loved Shaitan dearly and regarded him like her son, told him that he must take something home because he was going on leave around Diwali. She then went shopping with me in the local area market to buy shawls and other items for Shaitan's wife and family."

Mrs Khanna recalls with sadness how Shaitan Singh had to travel to Ladakh after his leave was cancelled just a few days before Diwali.

On October 24, Shaitan embarked on his journey to Leh along the same route as the battalion.

References

1. Interview with Mr Narpat Singh s/o Maj Shaitan Singh, PVC
2. Interview with Commandant Prithvi Singh (retd) Brother of Maj Shaitan Singh, PVC
3. Interview with Brigadier Raghunath V Jatar (retd)
4. Interview with Brigadier Prem Kumar (retd)
5. Interview with Honorary Captain Ram Chander, 13 Kumaon (retd)
6. Interview with Havildar Nihal Singh, 13 Kumaon (retd)
7. Telephonic Interview with Mrs Sheela Lamba w/o Brig B.S. Lamba
8. Telephonic Interview with Mrs Rani Khanna, w/o Maj Gen R.K. Khanna
9. Telephonic Interview with Mrs Pradanya Wakhle w/o Maj P.M. Wakhle
10. Telephonic Interview with Mrs Promila Soam d/o Lt Col Mukut Singh
11. Telephonic Interview with Lt Gen Ramesh Halgali (retd) s/o Maj G. Halgali
12. Interview with Mrs Sunita Mukherjee d/o Col H.S. Dhingra, AVSM
13. Interview with Major Haramrit Singh Dhingra (retd) s/o Col H.S. Dhingra, AVSM
14. Telephonic Interview with Col S.P. Dua (retd)
15. Letters of Major Shaitan Singh, PVC
16. Documents of Major Shaitan Singh, PVC

❑

The Dragon Strikes

The Sino-Indian War of 1962

13 Kumaon Headquarters at Chushul

In this chapter, the author has taken the liberty to write about the events which led to the Sino-Indian war of 1962. This chapter also discusses deployments and some major battles which took place in Daulat Beg Oldie, Galwan and Hot Springs in Ladakh front in October, 1962.

China unexpectedly and suddenly attacked India in October 1962. It quickly uprooted Indian barricades as it moved forward like an avalanche. And the Chinese frantically ended the conflict as they had started it. Many contend that China's ultimate objective in launching the attack was to dethrone India from its position as the leader of the Afro-Asian countries, which it had held since the early 1950s, and that the boundary disputes that preceded it were merely a pretext for it. Others contend that China wanted to undermine India's politics, democratic system, strength of its military, and quality of its training. There is no doubt that the invasion had a huge influence on India and its policymakers regardless of the reasons.

The relationship between China and India was friendly to begin with. India's first prime minister, Jawaharlal Nehru, liked China because it had suffered from foreign exploitation like India. He frequently stressed the two countries' long standing cultural ties.

Eighteen years before China attacked India and one year before India gained Independence, on September 7, 1946, Nehru, who was then the vice-president of the executive council of the Indian Interim National Government, in a radio address had said: "China, that enormous country with a mighty past, our neighbour, has been our friend throughout the years, and that friendship will survive and be offered."

However, this viewpoint was not shared by the Chinese leadership at that time and the leaders after Mao Zedong's communist takeover of the country. The Mao-led Chinese Communist Party leadership, who had overthrown the regime of Chiang Kai-shek, thought that the west, especially Britain, still had an influence on India. K.M. Panikkar, former Indian ambassador to China, wrote: "Mao opened the conversation by saying that in China, there was an old belief that if a man lived a decent life, he would be reborn in India. The first ten years of the People's Republic of China, which was established on October 1, 1949, saw cordial relations between China and India. The imperialists grew envious of this friendship between the two nations. The causes were plain to see. India was able to free itself from the burden of imperialism after a protracted battle and significant sacrifices. The emancipation of numerous Asian nations was made possible by India's anti-imperialist fight and eventual success. The people of China successfully carried out their revolution, which had its roots in the anti-imperialist movement, two years after India gained its freedom. Therefore, there was a basis for friendship between the two nations.

The People's Republic of China was established by the communists on October 1, 1949, under the leadership of Chairman Mao Zedong. One of the first nations to accept the new regime was India, which also used every opportunity in the years that followed to advance its case for UN membership. After that, China invaded Tibet in 1950. Indian opinion was shaken by it.

The primary source of concern in India was Chinese maps, which depicted significant portions of India's border regions as Chinese territory. There were over 50,000 square miles at stake. The issue of Tibet's neutrality was another. India and Tibet developed a unique relationship throughout the British era. Indian traders and pilgrims had easy access to Tibet, thanks to the Indian government's presence in Tibet, which included a mission in Lhasa and posts at Gyantse and Yatung. After the communist takeover of China, Chou En-lai, the Chinese premier, formally assured India's ambassador in Peking (now Beijing), in September 1951, that China intended to protect Indian interests in Tibet and added that "there was no territorial dispute or controversy between India and China." This put India's fears to rest.

The two governments negotiated an agreement in 1952 allowing the mission in Lhasa to continue. But because of the altered circumstances in Tibet, attempts by Indian traders, pilgrims, and intellectuals to visit Tibet in accordance with the longstanding tradition were frequently met with harassment. On April 29, 1954, following extensive negotiations, an agreement known as an Agreement for Trade and Cultural Intercourse was signed between India and China to resolve these issues. The five guiding principles (Panchsheel) for future ties between India and China were spelt out in the agreement's preamble. The pact was lauded as a significant step towards peaceful coexistence in both nations; Hindi-Chini Bhai-Bhai became an appealing slogan, and Panchsheel was praised as the ideal framework for international relations. The Indian government had already made it clear that it intended to renounce its extraterritorial claims to Tibet before the deal was even finalised. It gave the Chinese as a gesture of goodwill its postal, telegraph, telephone, and rest house facilities in Tibet the day after the agreement was signed.

According to K.M. Pannikar, the Chinese army had moved in on the entire boundary from Arunachal (then known as the North-East Frontier Agency or Nefa) to Ladakh by 1956 and had established posts at various places. The 2,200-mile border between Tibet and India thus became active after having remained dormant from time immemorial.

Less than three months after the agreement was signed, China made its first claims to Indian territory. The place in question was Barahoti, a trading post three miles inside the Indian border in Uttarakhand's Garhwal region, which was in undivided Uttar Pradesh at that time. Soon after, there were rumours that China had intervened in Aksai Chin's Ladakh region. On October 6, 1957, the Chinese officially declared the Sinkiang-Tibet Road complete. On a map published in their newspapers was the approximate routing of a road that traversed the Aksai Chin.

In the Aksai Chin, a high, arid plain with alkaline soil, the boundaries of Ladakh, Tibet, and Sinkiang meet. It was previously believed that this area was abandoned because it featured no floral diversity. As soon as the snow melted in 1958, India sent out small reconnaissance groups to ensure that the Chinese route passed through Indian territory. One of these parties was eventually apprehended by Chinese border guards, but another managed to complete the journey and return with information that Chinese forces were well-established in the Aksai Chin region. After India objected to the illegitimate invasion of its territory, the Chinese government declared possession of Aksai Chin. The path allowed China to take control of 12,000 square kilometres of Indian territory.

Something occurred in 1959 that worsened India-China ties and gave it a "new dimension". Lhasa was affected by the Khampa revolt in Tibet at the beginning of that year. To put an end to it, the Chinese embarked on a huge offensive. As a result, the Dalai Lama fled the Tibetan capital. He arrived in India on March 31, 1959, and was given refuge by the Indian authorities. Chinese propaganda against India became more aggressive, and in the months that followed, it became clear that China had expanded its military control over Ladakh. On July 28, Chinese troops camped out in Spanggur and captured a squad of Indian policemen who were conducting a reconnaissance patrol inside Indian territory. Nine Indian policemen were killed and seven were taken in a significant combat that took place at the Kongka Pass, 48 miles inside the Indian border, on October 21, 1959. Our border post in Arunachal, Longju, was taken over by the Chinese earlier in August.

In 1959, Chinese forces invaded Indian territory in Ladakh and killed local police officers. Police official Karam Singh was the first victim of the Chinese onslaught. He gave his life as a hero to protect the geographic integrity of the country. The border incident wasn't just a minor matter that could be disregarded. It was the beginning of a violent trend that had its roots in the China's leadership's expansionist policy towards a neighbouring country. If China had wished to instigate a conflict, India would have responded by ambushing the intruders. India only managed to deal with this situation by diplomatically expressing its concern to the Chinese leadership to persuade China to alter its policy of provoking conflict with India.

At the same time, steps were taken to prevent Chinese troops from further invading our territory. To signal possession, this involved creating numerous new outposts on the border, settling vantage points in wide-open places, and constructing roads to link the outposts to their bases under the new "Forward Policy."

The Army Takes Over

The Assam Rifles in Arunachal, armed police in the central sector, and the Jammu & Kashmir Militia in Ladakh had manned the India-Tibet border till that point. After these serious occurrences, the Army was asked to take control over the whole border, even though police or paramilitary men remained to guard the border crossings as they had in the past.

In 1960, the Army was given responsibility for the northern borders. This resulted in the induction of Brig Rawind Singh Grewal, MC, who led the 114 Infantry Brigade, which included the 7 J&K Militia and the 14 J&K Militia. The 1/8 Gorkha Rifles, led by Lt Col Hari Chand, MVC, became the force's third battalion in April 1961. These battalions were assigned to three different areas. The 14 J&K Militia oversaw the area north of the Galwan river. The 1/8 Gorkhas were responsible for the area between Galwan and Chushul, while the 7 J&K Militia were given the responsibility of the southern territory, consisting of the Indus Valley.

In April 1961, a platoon of the 14 J&K Militia was given the responsibility to establish a post at Daulat Beg Oldie, also termed the "Gateway to Hell" by old traders. It was 16 kilometres southeast of the Karakoram Pass. Survival in the terrain and severe weather was a tough challenge in this region, and the enemy came after that. In those days, Ladakh's connectivity was also very poor, with only a jeepable road connecting Chushul and Leh. Therefore, air supply was the only way to keep posts operational.

In the early stages of the 1962 India-China War, Ladakh had only four battalions: 1/8 Gorkha Rifles, 14 J&K Militia, 7 J&K Militia, and 5 Jat, led by Lt Col Bakhtawar Singh, which was inducted from Uri in June 1962, along with a company of 1 Mahar (MMG) under Major T.R. Reddy. These four battalions covered a front of 480 kilometres from DBO in the north to Demchok in the south.

Brig Rawind Singh Grewal was promoted and transferred for his new assignment in July 1962, and he was replaced by Brig Tapishwer Narain Raina, a Kumaoni officer who was fondly known as Tappy Raina.

The Battle in DBO Sector

In addition to the 14 J&K Militia, the 5 Jat's Charlie Company was also in the DBO sector. On the north and south banks of the Chip Chap river, 9 posts were established, and 5 posts were established opposite Murgo and Sultan Chushku. Every post had only five to 25 men.

All the posts were equipped with small arms and less ammunition compared to the enemy. On the eve of October 20, the Chinese troops at various locations in front of the Indian posts came with loudspeakers and warned the Indian troops to withdraw.

On the eve of the war's first day, the Chinese began to gather and bring heavy weaponry. At Qizil-Jilga, they had a regiment with two units for attacking and one reserved. Posts 5 and 9 were attacked at the same time on October 19 at around 11 pm.

Post 5 (named Pramodak) was the tiniest post in the sector, with only four men under Hav Tulsi Ram of 5 Jat. It was attacked by two Chinese companies, but due to the post's altitude, the men of 5 Jat dominated and held the post till the Chinese began shelling. Except for the non-commissioned officer (NCO), who decided to continue to operate the machine gun, all four men died. As his ammunition was running out, Tulsi Ram slipped out of the way with his gun and went downward to DBO. He was later awarded the Vir Chakra (VrC). Pramodak fell.

Post 9 was manned by 11 men from the 14 J&K Militia under the command of company Hav Maj Anant Ram and was under heavy mortar and medium machine gun (MMG) fire. The Chinese remained outside the range of the Indian weapons but were inflicting damage on the Indian side with their longer-range weapons. The Chinese shelled the post for nearly an hour, killing four men, before the infantry surrounded it. With his remaining men, Hav Anant Ram found an opening and managed to extract his men while inflicting heavy casualties on the Chinese soldiers. Hav Anant Ram was awarded the VrC for his bravery.

On October 20, both posts – 5 and 9 – fought till the first light of the morning. The Chinese occupied Post 5 and cut off the other posts' withdrawal and supply routes. Around 2.30am, the Chinese attacked posts 2 and 3, manned by the Jats, on the north bank of Chip Chap. However, after giving a solid fight to the Chinese, the men of these posts withdrew to Post 4.

Post 1 (named Chandni) was on high ground, which made it difficult for the enemy to fight. However, it was now isolated, as every post around it had been abandoned or occupied by the enemy. The post was manned by Subedar Sonam Stopdhan, who had 25 other ranks (ORs) from the 14 J&K Militia. On October 20, Chandni was heavily shelled and subjected to a large infantry assault. The officiating commander of DBO, Major Shardul Singh Randhawa, attempted to send reinforcements, but Chinese at other posts made it impossible. The Indian troops put up a heroic defence and stymied three attacks, but the Chinese outran them and overran the post, killing everyone on it. Chandni fell. When Maj Randhawa got this information, he passed the message to the brigade major, Jagjit Singh, in a very emotional voice. He said, "Chandni khatam ho gayi! Chandni jal gayi! (Chandni is finished. Chandni is burned down)." Sub Stopdhan was awarded the Maha Vir Chakra (MVC), and sepoys Chiring, Wangchuk, and Phunchok were awarded VrCs.

Post Bhujang, held by 15 men of the 14 J&K Militia under Nb Sub Rigzin Phunphok, had a similar story. His post was subjected to heavy shelling before being attacked by the Chinese infantry. The post fought valiantly, but it was vastly outnumbered. A few of the 15 men survived and fell back to Sultan Chushku. Hav Saroop Singh, who was killed in action at the post, was later awarded the MVC.

At 7 pm, on October 20, the Chinese began shelling Post 4, which had nearly 40 men and was in communication with the DBO OC, Maj Randhawa, who asked men of 5 Jat to return to DBO. However, due to the pitch-black night, only one JCO and nine other ranks (ORs) were found by the patrol sent from the DBO garrison.

By that time, only the post DBO garrison, which had 125 ranks, was constantly in contact with the 114th Brigade.

2/Lt Harish Chander Gujral was sent with reinforcements and relieved Lt Prem Singh on October 22 to take command of the forward post Arni-I in Ladakh and hold it until further orders. He broke through the enemy ring around the post with determination and courage, took reinforcements in, and reorganised the post's defence.

When he was ordered to leave, he had to fight his way out once more. Gujral was awarded the Vir Chakra for his gallant deed. (Later, in the 1965 war with Pakistan, the brave officer fought gallantly and fell fighting.)

Every post was heavily mortar-bombed by the Chinese. Until now, the Chinese had eliminated all the posts on Chip Chap's northern bank. Only Post 4 managed to resist. The Chinese posed a direct threat to the DBO and track junction with Post 5 in their hands.

Post 10 was attacked in large numbers, and they requested a withdrawal to Burtse, which was located north of Murgo. The enemy occupied the post. East of Murgo was Post Jodha, which was manned by a platoon of 14 J&K Militia and was attacked from the north on October 21. The post fought effectively but was surrounded by nearly two companies of Chinese soldiers. Three men were killed in action, four were wounded, and two were taken prisoner.

Except for isolated Post 14, Jyotish, all isolated posts were ordered to fall back to Burtse on the night of October 21.

The post commander reported heavy enemy concentrations opposite the post at 1pm, on October 21. Till now, Lt Col Nihal Singh, CO 14 J&K Militia, flew in from Thoise to DBO. Following his conversation with him, he ordered Post Jyotish to fall back on Sultan Chushku.

By this time, DBO was surrounded. Eighteen posts had fallen on October 20 and 21. On October 22, the battalion commander asked for a withdrawal from the brigade. Later, the corps issued an order to withdraw to a better defensive position. Maj Randhawa also conveyed a message via the pilot of the helicopter that the Chinese concentration could pose a serious threat to Leh.

At 6 pm, the brigade ordered the withdrawal of the 14 J&K Militia. The operation began at 9pm. The only route now left was a difficult western route through Gapshan, Shyok, and Saser Brangsa. To confuse and distract the Chinese who intercepted the radio communication, the battalion commander also sent a false message to the brigade.

Weapons and equipment, such as 3-inch mortars, recoilless guns, radio sets, and supplies, were destroyed by retreating troops. The Indian soldiers were now given personal weapons and 100 rounds each. A platoon of 1 Mahar (MMG) attached to the battalion under the command of Nb Sub Bhimu Kamble refused to destroy their guns and carried the weapons with them. It was a challenging retreat.

When Kamble learned that a gun from his platoon had been lost, he returned with his six men, despite the Chinese threat, and entered the abandoned post, grabbed the gun, and escaped unharmed.

There were only a few vehicles, including a few jeeps and one-tonne trucks loaded with sick and injured soldiers. These vehicles used the river's frozen surface, but the surface soon gave away due to the weight, and the vehicles had to be abandoned.

The retreat was divided into three parties, with the advance party led by Maj Randhawa, who was well acquainted with the routes and the men of his battalion. The main body was led by the CO, Lt Col Nihal Singh, and the rear party was led by Capt S.P. Rigzin. The rear party platoon occupied the dominant post and withdrew on the first light of October 23, while other troops were on their way to Saser Brangsa. Tired and carrying heavy loads, it was a test of the Indian troops' endurance and training.

After reaching Saser Brangsa, the casualties were evacuated by helicopter, and much-needed supplies were airdropped.

After October 23, there was no fighting in the DBO sector till the official ceasefire on November 21. The troops fought with grit, determination, and bravery. Maj Shardul Singh Randhawa, who was also awarded the MVC, deserves much of the credit for the successful retreat and operations in the DBO sector.

The Galwan-Chang Chenmo sector, or the middle sector, is located south of DBO and east of Shyok. The 1/8 Gorkha Rifles were in control of this sector. Higher officials decided to establish an isolated post deep within the Galwan valley in June 1962. On July 4, the commanding officer of 1/8 Gorkha Rifles, Lt Col Hari Chand, MVC, established a platoon-sized post opposite the Chinese post at Samzungling on orders from Army Headquarters. On July 10, around 300 Chinese surrounded the Galwan post, which was manned by Nb Sub Jang Bahadur and 30 ORs of 1/8 GR.

The Chinese had left the surrounding area the next day, but they were still close to the post. They continued to demoralise the troops with propaganda slogans. Maj V.P. Bhasin of the 1/8 Gorkhas arrived a few days later with a reinforcement column to strengthen the post. The Chinese used to cut off the supply route through the patrol base. Once they stopped a platoon-sized Yak-loaded supply patrol, they insisted the patrol return to the base immediately. No fire was exchanged during the incident.

After three months of deployment, the Gorkhas were relieved. Mi-4 helicopters were used for the relief operation. Brig Grewal had been transferred by the time the Gorkhas were relieved, and Brig T.N. Raina had taken over command of 114 Brigade.

The 5 Jat was ready for induction into the sector in the first week of October 1962. The Alpha Company of 5 Jat, comprising 60 men led by Maj S.S. Hasabnis, was chopper-lifted and flown to the Galwan post.

The Jats in Galwan faced numerous challenges. Snow began to fall, and the land route was completely cut off due to the Chinese posts. The post was completely dependent on air supplies, which only arrived when the weather was clear. Supplies would occasionally fall on the enemy side as well. The Chinese continued to harass the troops using propaganda slogans and encircled the post every now and then.

The Battle of Galwan

The Chinese bombarded the Galwan post with heavy artillery and mortar fire in the early hours of October 20, 1962. The intense shelling destroyed the post's tents and defences. After the shelling stopped, the Chinese infantry launched a battalion-sized assault on the forward defences. Those valiant Jats fought against their crumbling defences. Heavy weapons were not available to support the Indian troops.

Even after being injured, Sub Nihal Singh inspired his troops to fight till the bitter end. The troops continued to fight and resist, but the forward defences were eventually breached. Maj Hasabnis, in the rear position, continued to repulse Chinese attacks with his remaining troops.

After hours of fighting, the Chinese were able to capture the post, killing 36 Indian troops, including Capt (Dr) Paul of the AMC, out of 60 all ranks. Eighteen men were severely injured. The men fought till the last bullet was fired.

Those men, who knew death and defeat stared them in the eye, understood that there was no way out. But they did not raise the white flag of surrender. They were vastly outnumbered. The enemy forcibly captured Maj Hasabnis and his remaining troops.

When Indian helicopters flew over the Galwan post on October 21, they were fired upon by the Chinese troops. The pilot was unable to contact the post. When the pilot returned, he reported that there was no sign of life on the post. All the men were believed to be missing in action.

Chang-Chenmo Subsector

Following the fall of the Galwan post, the Chinese moved to the Chang Chenmo valley, which included strategically important posts, such as the patrol base, Nullah junction, and Hot Springs. The Chinese began shelling all the posts. Maj Ajit Singh's Bravo

Company was headquartered in Hot Springs and had platoon-sized posts at the patrol base, Nullah Junction, and the Hot Springs area.

Since Galwan had already fallen, it was no longer necessary to maintain the patrol base, which served only as a link between the Nullah junction and the Galwan post.

Patrol Base

Sub Amar Singh's post at the patrol base was ordered to withdraw and return to the Nullah junction. The Chinese began to heavily bombard the post. The platoon began to withdraw as soon as the sun set.

"We've come here to fight the Chinese," Amar Singh told his men. "Remember, no matter what, we are not leaving this sacred ground."

A section led by the subedar remained in the rear to observe and report on Chinese activity in the area. True to his words, Amar Singh stayed back.

The Chinese began shelling the section's posts on October 22 at 11.30 am. Amar Singh went to the observation post to assess the situation when the Chinese attacked the post, and after a while, the entire section was under attack. The subedar didn't try to escape. Instead, he continued to inspire his men to fight till the end.

The Chinese overran the post, killing the brave commander and nearly all the men. The patrol base was destroyed.

Kongma and Ane-La

A crucial position held by a platoon of Jat's Delta Company. The Delta Company, minus two platoons, was based at the battalion headquarters in Phobrang, which was led by Maj Sangram

Singh, another senior of Maj Shaitan Singh from the Kotah Umed Infantry. Kongma was a well-positioned post. On October 22, in broad daylight, 300 Chinese troops attacked the post. The post was heavily shelled before the infantry assault. The Indian soldiers manning the post were injured, and their defences were destroyed.

The first wave of Chinese attacked as soon as the shelling stopped. The valiant Jats fought back and repulsed the first attack. The Chinese kept coming in large numbers. The ammunition for the section's light machine gun had run out after a few hours of fighting. Nk Munshi Ram emerged from his trench with ammunition from the reserve. While returning to his trench, he was hit by a shell and was killed. Munshi Ram was posthumously awarded the Vir Chakra.

Sub Surjit Singh, the platoon commander, was hit by a burst and fell while moving from section to section, inspiring his men to fight till their last breath and last round. The fighting lasted several hours. Only seven men out of a total of 33 survived. The ammunition ran out, and the post collapsed, forcing the survivors to escape to battalion headquarters in Phobrang.

Ane-la held another Delta Company platoon post. It also came under artillery and mortar fire. The infantry attacked the post in waves, and the first few attacks were repulsed. The fighting lasted all night. But the Chinese eventually took over the post. The survivors were forced to abandon the post.

Kongma and Ane-la were now under Chinese control and posed a serious threat to the other Indian posts, as they could cut off Nullah Junction, Tsogt Salu, and Hot Springs.

Nullah Junction

The corps headquarters was informed of the fall of Kongma and Ane-la. After reviewing the situation, the corps commander, Lt

Gen Bikram Singh, issued orders to withdraw troops, including the Indo-Tibetan Border Police, to prepare rear defences at Tsogt Salu.

The Chinese shelling began in the late hours of October 23, as the withdrawal began. At this platoon-sized post, one section served as the observation post and suffered the most damage. After the Chinese infantry attacked the frontal section, the other two sections were ordered to retreat. The front section commander, Nk Maya Ram, kept fighting and covered the retreat with six of his men. Four of his comrades were killed in the fighting, and two were injured. When he realised he could not hold the post, he helped his wounded comrades extricate themselves, and then he himself abandoned the post.

Meanwhile, the 114 Brigade issued a new order, this time to abandon Tsogtsalu and return to the battalion headquarters at Phobrang. The withdrawal via Marsimik-la was impossible because the fall of Kongma and Ane-la threatened the route. As a result, troops were ordered to move along the Chang Chenmo river, keeping the threat in mind.

It was a difficult path to take. After crossing the inhospitable terrain, the troops arrived in Phobrang, and it is said that nearly all of them suffered frostbite or altitude-related sickness.

Hot Springs

Hot Springs, which was the Bravo Company's headquarters, was isolated while other posts withdrew. The brigade directed that the Hot Springs post withdraw and join the battalion, minus the Charlie Company, at Lukung.

Maj Gen Jagjit Singh, the-then brigade major of the 114 Brigade, wrote in his book: "I personally spoke with the company commander at Hot Springs when he received the orders to withdraw. He was extremely disturbed and kept insisting that this gave us a chance to avenge the massacre of our brothers elsewhere. Let Chinese blood flow at Hot Springs. We are well prepared, and my men are fully behind me."

After a while, numerous Chinese troops began to gather in front of the post, so Maj Ajit Singh was ordered to retreat as soon as possible to Lukung. The Bravo Company left Hot Springs, but the next day, on October 24, a platoon led by Sub Norang Lal reoccupied the Nullah junction and took control of Hot Springs as well. Ajit Singh received the Maha Vir Chakra for this action.

From Phobrang to Shyok, the 5 Jat began to fortify their defences. Even though Tsogtsalu was under Jat control, the Chinese didn't attempt to advance. Intense patrolling under Capt N.K. Chaudhary, Lt Prem Singh, Sub Norang Lal, and Nb Subedar Jai Lal dominated the area, and the sector remained occupied by the Jats. For his meritorious service, Sub Norang Lal was awarded the Vishisht Seva Medal. 2/Lt HC Gujral of 5 Jat at Arni-I in the DBO sector was awarded the Vir Chakra for his gallant actions.

A total of 200 men of all ranks were hospitalised, 53 killed in action, and 64 injured. Almost 60 men of all ranks were taken prisoner. They were returned on May 17, 1963.

The actions of the "Balwan" (valiant) Jats in the Galwan-Chang Chenmo sector remain unspoken, and their tales of valour and tenacity go untold. They were aware that they were isolated and outnumbered, but they refused to raise the white flag. Although some Jats still protect the sacred soil in the lap of the Himalayas, they were never found. They faced the bitter end with courage.

References

1. Interview with Mr Devraj Singh s/o Lt Col Bakhtawar Singh, 5 Jat
2. Interview with Subedar Balwant Singh, 5 Jat (retd)
3. Interview with Brigadier Raghunath V. Jatar (retd)
4. Interview with Brigadier Prem Kumar (retd)
5. Interviews with veterans of 5 Jat (all retd)
6. Interview with Mahendra Kanwar daughter-in-law of Lt Col Sangram Singh (retd)
7. Book: *Valour Triumphs: A History of the Kumaon Regiment Hardcover* by K.C. Praval
8. Book: The Saga of Ladakh by Maj Gen Jagjit Singh

❑

The Battle of Chushul

Maj Shaitan Singh, 13 Kumaon

The Chushul sector, this chapter not only gives a detailed version of the battle of Rezang La but also talks about the new deployments of 114 Brigade and the battle of Chushul. Here in this chapter the life of Major Shaitan Singh comes to an end but his story continues.

The Chushul sector, which is located south of the Chang-Chenmo valley and has the Pangong-tso (Pangong lake) as its main attraction, The village of Chushul is located to the west of the vast Spanggur Gap, which is located on the west side of the Spanggur lake and has a mountain slope on its south bank. The Chushul airstrip, which was established by Brig K. Bagh Singh in 1952, was strategically significant. It is located between the village and the Spanggur Gap. Here, An-12 and Packet planes used to land frequently.

Chushul was held by two companies of the 1/8 Gorkha Rifles when the conflict began. Delta Company, which was a platoon less, was led by Maj Dhan Singh. It was stationed at the Sirjap complex, which was maintained by assault boats and had no land connection to the Chushul garrison. The Yula complex, located south of Pangong, was manned by a company of 1/8 GR. The remaining two companies were sent to defend the Spanggur Gap. The company troops were positioned on the north and south shoulders of the Spanggur Gap, named Gurung Hill and Magar Hill respectively, with a post in the Spanggur Gap as well. Gurung Hill and Magar Hill were named after the main subcastes of the unit's troops.

Since September 1962, the Chinese had surrounded the Sirjap complex, which included the company positions Sirjap I and II. The Chinese were well prepared since it had direct road linkages to Sirjap with Khurnak fort, making it simpler for them to transport reinforcements, supplies, and heavy weaponry, but Indian forces only had personal weapons and LMGs, with the lake serving as the only supply line.

The Battle of Sirjap

Maj Thapa's company was in the Sirjap area, near the Pangong-tso, and was supplied and maintained by assault boats. The People's Liberation Army soldiers used artillery and mortars to attack the Indian Army position of Sirjap I early on October 21. Consequently, the Gorkha troops were severely injured. At this juncture, Chinese troops began to progressively approach the Indian stronghold. The Chinese soon came up with light tanks against which Indian troops had no weaponry. Then, the Chinese forces launched an overwhelming assault on Thapa's isolated company.

The Gorkhas responded valiantly with fortitude and repulsed three enemy attacks. Unfortunately, Thapa's company suffered greatly during this conflict, and just seven of his 28 troops survived. After a while when the Indian soldiers' ammunition ran out, the Gorkhas yelled their war cry "Jai Maa Kali Aayo Gorkhali" and attacked the Chinese with their khukris.

However, Sirjap I fell to the enemy due to the larger size of the enemy forces. After overpowering the Indian forces with their numerical superiority, the Chinese captured Thapa as a prisoner of war. Since there was no connection with the post, the battalion headquarters dispatched one patrol led by Nk Rabi Lal Thapa (who was later awarded the Maha Vir Chakra). The boat got as near as 1,000 yards to the position before being fired upon by the enemy. So it turned around and reported that the entire post had collapsed, assuming Thapa and his men had been killed.

Then, after a fierce battle, the Chinese also took over Sirjap II. And by October 22, all forward posts in the Chushul sector had been either withdrawn or overwhelmed by the enemy.

The Indus Valley

The Indus Valley is located south of Chushul in the southern sector. It was an important location since it had a route that connected Chushul to Dungti and then south to Demchok. Lt Col R.M. Banon, commanding officer of the 7 J&K Militia, was in charge of the subsector's defence. The unit had its headquarters in Koyul with a company, and troops of a company strength stationed in Dungti. The rest of the battalion was dispersed in small posts along the passes.

On October 27, the Chinese began attacking posts in the southern sector, following identical attack tactics which they used in the northern and the middle sector.

The Battle of Chang-La

The Chinese forces assaulted the Chang-la post on October 27. Indian soldiers, numbering just 17, held the post against the larger enemy and prevented the post from being captured. However, with ammunition running low and Chinese strength building, it was becoming harder to uphold the post. At one point, the post commander, who was a JCO, ordered his troops to withdraw while he provided cover fire with his LMG. The escaping troops made it to nearby Fukche. However, the post commander, who assisted his comrades in escaping, fell to enemy fire.

The Battle of Jara-La

The Chinese, together with Chang-la, encircled the post at Jara-la. There were also 17 men under the command of a non-commissioned officer (NCO). Over 300 Chinese troops marched up to the position and surrounded it in the morning. The Chinese encircled the post all day, but Indian troops managed to escape during the night, although one soldier was killed and seven were taken prisoner.

Other positions in the region were similarly besieged and overwhelmed by the Chinese. Sep Sonam Rabgais was on one of these posts when it was bombarded by the Chinese. He fought valiantly and remained in his trench till he was killed in action. He was later awarded the Vir Chakra.

Most of the Indian troops in the sector were asked to withdraw. The withdrawal commenced on the intervening night of October 27-28 and troops successfully managed to reach Koyul.

Induction of 13 Kumaon

On October 13, Bravo Company, under the command of Capt Hari Singh Chauhan, reached Chushul. The company was straightforwardly asked to scale Magar Hill post, which was formerly occupied by the troops of 1/8 Gorkha Rifles. The next company to reach Chushul was the Delta Company, which reached thereafter three days under the leadership of Capt Raghunath Jatar. Jatar was in Delhi to prepare for his upcoming exam to enrol in the Staff College. When he got to know about the paltan's move to Ladakh, he stopped his preparations and joined the unit. The Delta Company occupied the Spanggur Gap with one of its platoons holding Rezang-la.

The 13 Kumaon's battalion headquarters was under Lt Col H.S. Dhingra, who was accompanied by Lt P.M. Wakhle as his intelligence officer (IO). The Alpha and Charlie Companies came to Chushul on October 26. The battalion headquarters was located just near the Chushul airstrip, and the Alpha Company, under the command of 2-IC Maj G.N. Sinha, was made the brigade reserve.

The Charlie Company, under the leadership of Lt Prem Kumar, was sent to Rezang-la on October 27, and with this, the whole Delta Company was asked to climb Magar Hill. The Bravo Company and Delta Company (without a platoon) together held the Paw Hill and Magar Hill.

Most of the Indian troops in the southern sector were asked to withdraw. The withdrawal commenced on the intervening night of October 27 and 28. The troops successfully managed to reach Koyul.

On the same day, Maj Shaitan Singh and the battalion rear party reached Leh. He and his troops were asked to acclimatise. By this time, the first phase of the war was over in all the sectors.

Lt Prem Kumar was to lead the troops of the Charlie Company to Rezang-la. At this point of time, the Charlie Company had some 60-odd soldiers and only one JCO, Jem Surja Ram. The company began climbing Rezang-la, which is a massive feature of approximately 5,180 metres high. The troops were having difficulty climbing despite being acclimatised. After four hours of climbing, the troops and Lt Prem reached the Rezang-la post.

After reaching the pass, the company was asked to rest for the day. It was known to everyone that the first night was to be spent in the open without much bedding. Also, there was no proper equipment to cook food, so troops were asked to eat their dry rations.

By this time, the brigade headquarters had also moved to Chushul from Leh.

Initially based in Leh, Brig T.N. Raina-led Brigade was responsible for a vast frontage stretching from Daulat Beg Oldie to Demchok with just two regular infantry battalions and two J&K Militia battalions. It had no artillery or armoured support. Nevertheless, with the formation of the 3 Himalayan Division under Maj Gen Budh Singh, MC, on October 26, with the 70 Infantry Brigade and 163 Infantry Brigade under its command. The sector also received one field artillery regiment, two tank troops, one heavy mortar battery, and field engineers.

The Leh sector, which had previously been the headquarters of the 114 Brigade, was now under the command of 163 Infantry Brigade, which had one field battery with regimental headquarters, one troop of heavy mortars, and one engineer company.

The 114 Brigade's area of responsibility was reduced. Its operational area was now around 80 kilometres long, stretching from Lukung to Tsaka-la.

Now the 14 J&K Militia, which was formerly under 114 Brigade and was responsible for the northern sector, or Saser-la-Shyok-Thoise, directly came under the command of 3 Division.

New Deployment of 114 Brigade

During the lull, the geography of the deployments changed considerably.

The central or middle sector was held by the 114 Brigade, which was in charge of the Lukung—Chushul—Tsaka-La stretch. With three regular infantry battalions: 1/8 GR, 5 Jat, and 13 Kumaon. With two tank troops of 20 Lancers, the 38th field battery of the 13 Field Regiment, one troop of 32 Heavy Mortar, one company of field engineers, and one company of 1 Mahar (MMG), with all this force, the Brigade was now in a strong position.

The Southern Sector, which included Demchok-Dungti, was now under the command of Brig Rawind Singh Grewal, MC, who led the 70 Infantry Brigade with three infantry battalions and the 7 J&K Militia battalion, as well as one battery of the Field Regiment, one heavy mortar troop, one company of engineers, and one company of MMGs.

5 Jat under Lt Col Bakhtawar Singh, which had been hard-hit and sustained casualties in the DBO and Galwan sectors, was now regrouped and strengthened by troops from the Jat Regimental Centre and other sister battalions. The Battalion was now based in Lukung-Phobrang, and its alpha company, with fewer troops, was sent to Tsaka-La, which was adjacent to Rezang La, under the command of Lt Prem Singh. The battalion was also supported by a troop of 32 heavy mortar batteries.

1/8 Gorkha Rifles under Lt Col Hari Chand, VrC, the first battalion to move to Ladakh in 1961, was now without its Delta Company, which they lost in the Battle of Sirjap, and was given the responsibility of having one company each at Gurung Hill, Table Top-Camel's Back, and Spanggur Gap.

Y Company of 1 Mahar (MMG), under Maj T.R. Reddy, was part of the Brigade for a long time; it had participated in the first phase of DBO; now it moved to Chushul and was located at important positions, including Tsaka La.

20 Lancers, Following the spread of word that the Chinese were operating tanks in the region, the Indian Army began to induct tanks to confront the Chinese threat. Lt Col Gurbachan Singh 'Butch," who commanded 20 Lancers based in Ferozepur, was chosen for the assignment, and two tank troops with Squadron HQs were transported to Chandigarh Air Base, from where the tanks were to be flown in recently inducted AN-12 aircraft of the Indian Air Force's 44 Squadron. The trial to load tanks into aircraft began; however, due to the weight and structure of the tanks, the first trial failed, damaging the aircraft. With the assistance of local carpenters, a suitable ramp, adequate floor, and tail support for aircraft were quickly constructed, with sandbags acting as shock absorbers. Squadron Leader Chandan Singh, an accomplished aviator, was responsible for landing the tanks at Chushul Airbase. With the additional load from the tanks in mind, he took the risk and cut the aircraft fuel in half to finish the Chandigarh-Chushul-Chandigarh flight. He successfully landed the tanks at Chushul without any damage to the aircraft.

The squadron commander and two other officers were evacuated shortly after landing at Chushul owing to high altitude sickness, but Lt Avinash Chand, a tank commander, refused to be evacuated. Capt Ashwani Kumar Dewan was now in command of both the troops and the squadron headquarters. The tanks were now positioned near the foot of Gurung Hill, in a position where the enemy couldn't see them. That was the first time Indian tanks had been transported to such altitudes. It was extremely difficult to operate tanks owing to the weather and a lack of oxygen.

13 Field Regiment, Lt Col Shri Dhar Man Singh's Artillery Regiment, which was stationed somewhere in the Kashmir Valley, was asked to move quickly by road from Srinagar to Leh. The

regiment was headquartered in Leh, and its two batteries were transported to Chushul and Dungti under the 114 Brigade and 70 Brigade, respectively. Maj S.P. Joshi led the 38th Field Battery, which was moved to Chushul. The battery had two troops, each with four 25-pounder guns.

Brig Raina had asked for the plan of appreciation to position guns in Chushul from Maj S.P. Joshi. Maj S.P. Joshi had proposed to position one gun behind Rezang La, two guns behind Magar Hill, two guns in the Gap, and the rest behind Gurung Hill. But the positioning of the guns was changed by the commander, as he was aware that the Chinese would attack Magar Hill and Gurung Hill, not Rezang La.

All the guns were positioned at the base of Gurung Hill and Magar Hill to support both the hill features and the Spanggur Gap. Rezang La was left isolated since the gun behind Magar Hill was unable to support it owing to crest clearance issues. The battery had two observation posts, one at Gurung Hill and the other at Magar Hill, with Capt A.D. Singh and Capt Sharma being the OP officers.

With its two battalions, which incurred serious casualties in the initial phase of the war, and 14 J&K Militia, which had been placed directly under the command of 3 Div, and 7 J&K Militia, which had been transferred under the command of 70 Infantry Brigade. The 114th Brigade was short on manpower. With the addition of support components and two additional infantry battalions, the brigade quickly gained strength, and the commander began reconnaissance and siting operations.

The Charlie Company at Rezang La started to dig trenches and defences. The least exertion put them out of breath; while walking, the legs felt limp as if one were walking in a dream, and one had to pause after every half a dozen strokes with a pick or shovel. The company was to be deployed over a stretch of about 2 kilometres. The company consisted of Nos. 7, 8, and 9 platoons. The ground required to be covered at Rezang La was much larger than what could be covered by the troops available.

The No. 7 Platoon position was sited on the north flank, below the Mukhpari top. No. 8 platoon was positioned at the pass area, or the right flank. The centre area was given to No. 9 Platoon, with a suitable location for company headquarters near it. Now was the time to choose a position for the 3-inch mortar. Lt Prem Kumar, who had no experience leading mortar troops, was having difficulty finding the perfect location for the mortar section.

The company's administrative base, with its cook house, reserve rations, and clothing, was located at the Nullah below. The company position had been prepared well within the time limits and resources available.

Duty Comes First Always and Every Time

At Chushul High Ground, Maj Shaitan Singh and the rear party reached the Battalion Headquarters on October 30. His leave was cancelled for the time being. It made him sad as a family man but for a soldier his duty was his first priority even before his family.

He reached Chushul, which took him back to his days as a second lieutenant. Maj Shaitan Singh was the only officer in 13 Kumaon at the time who had experienced such weather and terrain before. He was posted with Kotah Umed Infantry at Dras, which is the second-coldest inhabited place on earth.

Battalion commander Lt Col H.S. Dhingra had instructed him to hand over the QM duties to Capt Gurdeep Singh, who was already officiating as the unit's QM. In the evening, Maj Shaitan Singh, Jem Hari Ram, Jemadar Ram Chander, and some troops without any acclimatisation in the valley were sent to Rezang La.

On reaching Rezang La, the Major took over charge of the Charlie company from Lt Prem Kumar.

The first thing he did was address his jawans. Sep Ram Chander, who was the radio operator at company headquarters, was appointed to be Maj Shaitan Singh's batman. The night fell, and it was certainly very cold. Troops who recently joined the company faced high altitude sickness.

The next day, Maj Shaitan Singh, who was a sound tactician and experienced mortar platoon commander, sited his company's 3-inch mortar position some 150 yards from company headquarters on the reverse slope under the leadership of Nk Ram Kumar, who had recently faced a demotion from the rank of Havildar due to disciplinary action taken against him.

The Major then took a trip to No. 9 platoon, which was led by Jem Ram Chander, followed by No. 7 platoon, that was sited on the north flank, where he met Jemadar Surja Ram. Then he went to No. 8 platoon, which was located on the right flank under Jemadar Hari Ram.

During this trip, Shaitan heard about issues faced by the jawans and the JCOs.

The ration potatoes were frozen when they arrived. The cooks could not peel them, nor could they cut them up; all they could do was smash them with the hammer. Luscious oranges sent up by the quartermaster proved equally obstinate. The peel came off in crusty bits, like the shell of a boiled egg; the inside was a ball of ice. Two stoves under a kettle of water for tea could not bring it to the boil for hours. The most trying feature of life on Rezang La was, however, the icy wind that sprang up daily, like clockwork, around midday and continued till late into the night.

The next day, on November 1, the CO was to visit Rezang La for an inspection of the positions of the platoons and troops readiness to face any upcoming attack. The company was prepared for the inspection, as the CO was greeted at the company headquarters by Maj Shaitan Singh and Lt Prem Kumar. The CO took Shaitan with him for the inspection, and Shaitan briefed him precisely about every possible enemy approach. Many gullies ran from the upper reaches of Rezang La towards Rezang Lungpa, two sandy tongues of the Spanggur Tso. These were likely approaches for the enemy.

He also showed CO the defences, which were still under preparation by the company. Shaitan also asked the CO to send adequate supplies for the troops, as they were facing problems. After the inspection, the CO instructed Lt Prem Kumar to move with him to Battalion Headquarters, from where he was to be sent to Magar Hill as a platoon commander. Now Charlie Company was left with 1 officer, 3 JCOs, and 127 other ranks.

It did not take long after CO's visit for the situation to improve when better equipment, canned food, and nourishing beverages reached Rezang La. Company HQs with overhead protection were soon ready, and the battalion had provided Charlie Company with three additional light machine guns to cover the gullies.

On November 2, 1 Jat (LI), the battalion, which was in the same formation as 13 Kumaon in Uri Sector, was given the order to move on very short notice. In just a few days, the entire battalion assembled at Srinagar Air Base, from where they were flown and transported to Chushul under the command of Lt Col Jaspal Singh. After being inducted into the sector on November 5 without acclimatisation, troops began to experience difficulties; shortly, a JCO died of altitude sickness, and the CO had to be evacuated the same day due to pulmonary edoema. Maj Balbir Singh who was the second-in-command of 5 Jat was the senior most in the hierarchy of both the Jat battalions in the sector so, later he was promoted to the rank of Lt Col appointed to command 1 Jat (LI). Alpha company was led by Capt Kuldeep

Singh Kang, who was also serving as the unit's adjutant, and Charlie Company, commanded by Maj Ranjit Singh Mavi, were deployed at Brigade Depth near the Battalion HQs at Chushul. Bravo company, commanded by Lt Surjit Singh Kaler, was deployed at Thankung and Yula, while delta company, commanded by Maj Sukhwinder Singh Malik, was stationed at Lukung on the shores of Pangong Tso.

On November 5, the brigade commander, Brig T.N. Raina, was supposed to come for an inspection with the Commanding Officer, Lt Col H.S. Dhingra, accompanied by the Brigade Major, Maj Jagjit Singh. The commander wanted to visit the location to get a first-hand view of the preparations and defences prepared by the charlie company before the corps commander's visit. In the hours of noon, the brigade commander reached Rezang La, sitting on the back of a mule. He got down and was greeted by Maj Shaitan Singh. The brigadier asked for his binoculars to see the Chinese movement near Spanggur Lake. He was later briefed about the preparations for defence and the ammunition. He also took an inspection trip to all the platoons and had tea with the officers present at the company headquarters.

On November 6, the corps commander, Lt Gen Bikram Singh, was scheduled to visit Chushul and meet the brigade commander with all the commanding officers. Before that, Lt Col Dhingra had called for an O group meeting, where all four company commanders—the Adjutant, Quartermaster, and IO—were to meet the CO. The meeting started with the CO's address to the officers, followed by the promotion of Capt Jatar to the field rank of Maj. He was also appointed Magar Hill post commander.

The conference continued, and Maj Shaitan once raised his voice over the lack of defence material like artillery support, mines, MMGs, and defence stores for constructing bunkers. The commanding officer also raised his voice and promptly silenced him. The atmosphere of the meeting was spoiled as everyone witnessed Maj Shaitan Singh raising his voice for the first time. The meeting soon ended.

After the meeting, Maj Shaitan met each of the officers personally and apologised for spoiling the atmosphere of the meeting! His demand was perfectly legitimate, but then that was his mindset as a perfect gentleman. Maj Shaitan was later met by Maj Sangram Singh, the Delta Company commander of 5 Jat who was his senior from the Kotah Umed Infantry. His company bravely fought in the Chang-Chenmo Sector and put up a great fight against the enemy in the first phase of the war before retreating to Lukung. Maj Sangram was due for his promotion to the rank of Lt Col and he was asked to move to Bareilly to raise the Seventh Battalion the Jat Regiment on November 15. He in a goodwill gesture exchanged his cane with Shaitan Singh's. The cane remained with Lt Col Sangram till he breathed his last in Jodhpur some 40 years after the war.

Later, Charlie company received some more supplies, which made the company much stronger. The platoon positions were now wired and stocked with six first-line scales of ammunition, and Nk Ram Kumar's mortar section had 1,000 bombs on hand. Thus, within the resources available, everything had been done to make Rezang La a well-defended post, though it suffered from certain disadvantages. One of these was nature's doing: due to an intervening feature, most of Rezang La was 'crested' to our artillery gun positioned below Magar Hill. But till that time, Maj Shaitan had sited everything very strategically. All his subunits were very well connected, and they were sited in such a position that the enemy could easily get tangled in crossfire.

Letters from the War

The letter written to Shri Govind Singh, brother of Lt Col Mal Singh, AC III by Maj Shaitan Singh dated November 7, 1962

My dear Govind Singh ji

Jai Shri Krishan

Thank you very much for your kind letter of October 30 which I received only yesterday.

You are quite correct in your assumption regarding my leave. Don't worry it is not that important. I shall have no regrets if I do not get leave. Duty comes first always and every time.

One thing I may write to you that I am in excellent health and wonderfully high spirits. Please don't bother about me ever.

I am in receipt of a letter from Malji. I have already replied to him. He is a wonderful person as far as I am concerned. Write to Malji to send me sweets in advance for his fourth to twelfth daughters. Don't you think it is a wonderful idea?

Where is Suganji–my love to her. Write me honestly- have you been blessed with a sweet child. Don't feel shy. My regards to Mrs. Govindsinghji. Please convey my regards to Khet Singhji and all those who know me.

With best wishes and good luck

Yours

Shaitan Singh

Letter written to Lt Col Mal Singh, AC III dated November 11, 1962

"My dearest brother,

Jai Ambe,

You wrote me this letter immediately after you recovered slightly and that too with your left hand; your right hand being unable to function for the present shows not only immense love and affection, you have for me but also your greatness. I am really very proud of you as a friend and brother."

"I believe they did not or ráther could not take out quite a few bullets from your body at Jamnagar, have they been pulled out now?"

Yours

Shaitan Singh

Last letter of Maj Shaitan Singh to his family dated November 13, 1962

My Dear Mr. Mool Singhji Sahib,

How fortunate I am to receive your most affectionate letter only yesterday.

I may assure you that I am in the best of health and in wonderfully high spirits.

I am where you think me to be, I may assure you I am really proud and happy to be here. We are all happy and there is no cause of any anxiety.

How are my sisters?

Kindly convey my regards and blessings to both of them and love to all youngsters (Ganshyam and Co).

How is your health and how is everyone? Kindly convey my regards to Shri Parbat Singh ji. Is he at Bawri or at Jodhpur?

Received two letters from Suraj and replied to them. No letter from either Lal or Prithvi. I wish and pray they are happy and healthy.

Where is your mother? Kindly convey my regards to her.

Any news from home? How were the crops at your villages? Any fresh news of interest?

Kindly convey my regards to your friends in office and muhalla.

I once again thank you very much for your affectionate letter and I would again like to assure you that I am most happy, healthy and in wonderfully high spirits.

With kindest regards

Yours sincerely

Shaitan Singh

Throughout the lull, no aggressive activity from the enemy side was recorded in November; however, they had a buildup at Spanggur Lake, which was connected by road from Rudok and Khurnak Fort, making it simpler for them to transfer weapons and supplies. Chinese preparations continued. Day after day, our observation posts watched their buildup. Their trucks came right up to their post at Spanggur. They did a lot of blasting, and their boats were seen plying on the Spanggur Tso at night. The area that seemed to get the most attention from them was the Spanggur Gap. Chinese parties would come up, spread out maps, take a good look, and go back. It was, in fact, the obvious route for attack, and we had laid anti-tank mines on it and covered it with RCL guns and artillery.

The Battle of Rezang La

The lull was not going to last for long. On November 17, 1962, Maj Shaitan Singh read and re-read a letter from his home in

Jodhpur and could not stop smiling. That snowy November night atop Rezang La in Chushul, he was amused to read about the rumours of his martyrdom. At 1900 hours, when Adjutant 13 Kumaon Capt D.D. Saklani, posted at the battalion headquarters, spoke to Singh, he shared his joke.

"Though he found it funny, he could sense some concern in his voice. Three hours later, he called him back to ask if he wanted to send a message back home, but by then the call operator said he had retired for the day. He did not want to disturb him. That was his last call to the Charlie Company on November 17. The late Lt Gen D.D. Saklani recounted this in an article.

On the night of November 17–18, the visibility was very low. It was only early in the morning when visibility improved to 600 metres. At 0400 hours, L/Nk Brij Lal at the listening post ahead of 8 Platoon observed a large body of Chinese soldiers swarming through the gullies at about 700–800 metres from the pass. L/Nk Brij Lal, the LP commander, ran back to Platoon Headquarters to inform them of this unusual development. He, his Section Commander Hukam Chand, and one LMG were rushed as reinforcements to the post. By then, the Chinese had advanced within firing range of small arms from the post. The LP fired a predetermined red very light signal along with long bursts of LMG fire, warning the C Company to 'stand to' in their dug-out positions.

After the eight-day battle, which concluded on October 27, there was a bizarre silence in Ladakh till the early hours of November 18. Suddenly, a bullet was fired and it broke the silence, ushering in some of the most famous battles in military history.

Similarly, 7 Platoon's LP on the forward slopes also saw the Chinese forming up, and the entire C Company was alerted. Maj Shaitan Singh immediately contacted his sub-unit commanders on the radio, who confirmed that all ranks were ready in their battle positions. Since the paucity of troops had caused wide gaps in 7 and 9 Platoon localities, he also ordered 9 Platoon to send a patrol to ascertain the situation. The patrol confirmed massive Chinese buildup had taken place through the gullies.

All ranks of the Charlie Company, with their fingers on triggers, waited patiently for the impending major frontal attack on their positions around first light, with improving visibility. Around 0500 hours, the first wave of the Chinese were spotted through their personal weapon sights by every Ahir manning the defences, and a hail of LMGs, MMGs, and mortar fire greeted the enemy. Scores of the enemy died; many were wounded, but the rest, duly reinforced, continued to advance as the Chinese believed in numbers and not changing strategies. Soon, all the gullies leading to Rezang La were full of Chinese corpses. Wave after wave of the Chinese launched four more attacks that were beaten back and dwindled the defender's strength and ammunition as many Ahirs fell fighting. As the fifth attack was launched, Nk Singh Ram, a wrestler of repute, led his comrades with a bayonet charge, killing 6-7 Chinese single-handedly till he fell to martyrdom. By about 0545 hours, the Chinese frontal attack had been beaten back and failed.

By now, the Chinese realised Rezang La was not a cakewalk and changed their plan. Rezang La resorted to heavy artillery shelling supported by three types of mortar: 120 mm, 81 mm, and 60 mm. To destroy field fortifications, they used concentrated fire of 75 mm and 57 mm recoilless (RCL) guns brought on wheelbarrows from the flanks and 132 mm rockets.

The shelling was indeed a spectacular display of Chinese might. Now they had also started shelling Gurung Hill, Magar Hill, and the 13 Kumaon Battalion HQs.

The shelling was so tremendous that it shook everyone located at Chushul. The Brigade Commander asked his Brigade

Major Jagjit Singh to take out his jeep so that he could have a first-hand experience of everything going on in the field.

Lieutenant Prem Singh, commanding Alpha Company of 5 Jat, watched it from Tsaka La, four miles away. 'I saw missiles 'with flaming red tails falling on Rezang La. To me and my company, the spectacle was so weird; we thought the entire Rezang La feature was on fire. He contacted the battalion commander and reported this to him. Later, the battalion commander tried to contact the Charlie Company, but he realised that the communication line had been cut off by the enemy.

A Naik of the Jammu and Kashmir Militia, at a post four miles south of Taska La, near Dungti, reported: "The explosions were so great that the walls of our cookhouse collapsed."

Between the shelling and the fifth wave of the infantry attack, Maj Shaitan Singh, who was going from company headquarters to No. 9 Platoon, was hit by enemy bullets in his left arm, but without caring about his own safety, he continued to fight and moved from one position to another. Realising the injury to the company commander, Sep Ram Chander took out his field bandage and insisted that Shaitan Singh should wrap it around.

The Chinese started regrouping for a rear attack on the 7th Platoon positions, which had been wiped out and had no survivors. A short distance away, Nk Sahi Ram, the only survivor detached from his platoon, waited for the enemy to assemble and let them have it with accurate LMG fire. The Chinese dispersed, and Sahi Ram waited for the next wave that came with RCL guns and blasted his lone firing position. Maj Shaitan Singh regrouped his dwindling assets to charge the advancing Chinese and asked his radio operator to check for any survivors. Since all the platoon positions had been overrun with no survivors, the enemy was regrouping to assault the C Company Headquarters from the rear after heavy pounding. Sep Nihal Singh, who was in his position manning the LMG and killing the enemy, just turned towards the No. 7 platoon position to shoot at the advancing enemy. Two bullets pierced his arms and got out, leaving holes. His arms were disabled, and the Chinese soldiers captured him.

He Got Killing Bullets

While moving from one gun position to another, motivating his men, a burst of medium machine gun brought by the enemy on a wheelbarrow from the paltoon 8 position hit Maj Shaitan in the left side of the abdomen. He did not realise that he was severely injured this time till he tried to run to another gun position and fell down. His limbs were now not supporting him due to continuous blood loss. With every drop of blood, life was ebbing out of him. He was seen by the remaining two men, Hav Jai Narain and Hav Phool Singh, who picked him up, and Maj Shaitan Singh asked them, "I want to throw up; put me down". Both men had till now realised that Major's abdomen had been slit open by the burst and that his intestines had come out of the body. They were shocked to see their company commander in such a condition and continued to rush downhill towards the company base, now and then taking cover behind boulders to escape the Chinese fire.

Maj Shaitan Singh had become unconscious with the loss of blood. Life was fast ebbing out of him. For a moment, he regained consciousness. Turning to the loyal jawans who risked their lives trying to carry him, he said, "Leave me alone and give me a weapon. Save your lives; I will not make it. It's an order," the Major said in a broken voice.

Reluctantly, the men obeyed and sat him behind a boulder with a gun. Sep Ram Chander, who was in search of survivors, now reached the company commander, who was still gasping for breath. The commander asked him to open his belt as it was hurting him so much, but when Ram Chander tried to put his hand inside the thick coat to open the belt, he could actually touch the Major's intestines. He rapidly removed his hand and told the Major that he could not open his belt. The Major asked him to leave and save his life.

No one knows when the Major breathed his last. But as much as I know him, he certainly would have smiled a little and thought of his company, which put up such a fierce fight against the mighty enemy, and for sure he would have remembered the line that was told to him during his junior command that he lacked assertiveness in his leadership and needed to improve his self-confidence. The thought of his school teacher saying to him, "Ek din yeh bohot badi shaitani karega," would have crossed his mind.

The last thought that passed his mind before breathing the last would certainly be of his family—his wife and son, whom he wanted to celebrate Diwali with but couldn't.

"Tell the CO and the battalion how well the company fought," were the last words heard from this brave soldier. With this, he breathed his last. The snowy pinnacles of Rezang La stood helplessly by watching this unequal match of 'so few against so many'. It was all over by about 9 am.

CHM Harphool Singh led three survivors to fight and stop the enemy's onslaught until martyred. Ram Kumar's 3-inch mortar section, having coughed up all its ammunition, was ordered to be disabled and fire plans and maps destroyed, lest they fall into Chinese hands. As Nk Ram Kumar disabled his mortars after raining 993 bombs on the enemy, he was hit by rifle fire from the Chinese 20 yards away. Though wounded, he took position in his command post, and as the Chinese peeped in, he pumped bullets with his bolt action. 303 rifle and killed many of them. The remaining Chinese hurled hand grenades to silence him and left. After many hours of profuse bleeding, he regained consciousness. The silence of war engulfed Rezang La as the last round was fired and the last soldier bled to martyrdom.

Neither help nor reinforcements were asked for, nor could any be provided to the Charlie Company.

Charlie Company's soldiers kept their promise of fighting till the last bullet and last breath.

Nk Ram Kumar, his body ridden with bullets and his nose blown off due to a grenade blast, could be seen coming down from Rezang La. Two men in a jeep of 13 Kumaon could see a person approaching them. Firstly, they thought he was Chinese, so they aimed at him, but Ram Kumar shouted with his arms raised in the air. He reached the jeep and told the soldiers about his condition. They carried him in the jeep and took him to the Battalion Headquarters to narrate the chilling story of the Rezang La Battle. Sep Ram Chander, who was the radio operator for Maj Shaitan Singh, reached the battalion headquarters after a few hours. He was the only unhurt soldier who came back. He was produced in front of the CO. He told everything that happened at Rezang La, but CO couldn't believe that such a fierce fight took place. No one could believe that Ram Kumar and Ram Chander had engaged in such a fierce fight.

Out of a total of 127 all ranks, one officer, two JCOs, and 106 other ranks laid down their lives. Every single man at Rezang killed 3-4 enemy troops. One JCO and five ORs were taken prisoner. Of the five prisoners, one later succumbed to his wounds. Only four managed to return alive from the ghastly hell at Rezang La on November 18. It is said that the battle had 17 survivors.

At Magar Hill, Bravo and Delta Company and the Battalion Headquarters had lost touch with Rezang La, so Maj Jatar sent a four-man patrol led by an NCO to investigate what had occurred there. Nonetheless, the Chinese surrounded the patrol and killed two men before they reached Rezang La; the remaining two men, however, managed to escape and reach their company position.

The Battle of Gurung Hill

Gurung Hill was a significant feature, measuring 3000 metres in length and 2000 metres in breadth, and 5030 metres high. It overlooked both the airstrip and the Spanggur Gap, and was divided into two sections: Camel's back and the tabletop. 1/8 Gorkha Rifles deployed its Bravo Company, less a platoon at the table top and a platoon at Camel's Back. 2/Lt S.D. Goswami and his three soldiers manned the Indian Artillery observation position on the hill. On November 18th, Chinese heavy artillery and mortar fire pounded Gurung Hill, but the enemy bombardment was less successful than at Rezang La.

The Gorkhas waited for the enemy to get within their firing range when Artillery OP 2/Lt S.D. Goswami got involved and was given a high level of responsibility. He kept bringing accurate fire to the Chinese, which effectively prevented them from advancing. Jem Tej Bahadur Gurung took over the leadership when post commander Capt P.L. Kher was wounded and continued battling and repelling the enemy, with the enemy suffering severe fatalities. Jem Tej Bahadur was wounded in the chest by a burst of fire while moving from one position to another, but he refused to be evacuated and fell down fighting. The Gorkhas were ordered to withdraw at Table Top due to their outnumbered position.

Capt P.L. Kher requested artillery support and direct fire from the tanks. Shyamal was severely wounded while bringing artillery fire on the enemy, and his technical assistant Gurdeep was shot and killed on the spot. Despite his injuries and heavy bleeding, Shyamal grabbed his radio and screamed "Fire Till Eternity" to his battery of guns. The Chinese arrived at his post to look for survivors, but assumed he was dead and abandoned the post. Shyamal regained consciousness a day later and crawled towards the base when two Gorkha troops spotted him and carried him to medical assistance. He was declared dead, but there was movement in his body, and he was sent to the Military Hospital in Delhi and later to Germany for rehabilitation after an amputation.

During the Battle of Gurung Hill, the artillery fired constantly, but the enemy soldiers did not approach the Magar Hill stronghold. Despite the fact that the enemy mercilessly bombarded the post. The Magar Hill also possessed an artillery OP, but no OP officer was present during the battle day; thus, the post commander, Major Jatar, directed artillery fire on the enemy in the immediate vicinity and the Spanggur Gap. Maj Jatar had the satisfaction of seeing the enemy and APCs fleeing back.

With the fall of Rezang La, there was a threat of an attack on the Chushul-Dungti track. The CO 13 Kumaon discussed the threat of an attack during the night with the brigade commander, and the commander decided to send one tank troop at last light, which would return to its hiding position by first light. Lt Avinash Chand arrived at 13 Kumaon's HQs just before dusk with one troop and a tank; he left the troop there and returned to repair the stalled tank. He returned to the reentrant and reported that there had been no Chinese activity in the region all night.

Attack on Camel's Back

The Chinese attacked the Camel's Back in 2030 hours on November 19 from two prongs: the Table Top, a former Gorkha position, and the Spanggur Gap. Due to the absence of the OP party, the fire was not precise, and the enemy overran the Camel's Back in less than an hour. The enemy suffered huge casualties, but the Gorkhas also suffered 26 casualties and several wounded out of total 102 all ranks. The battle of Gurung Hill was over. After the fall of Gurung Hill to the enemy, the Indian Air Force's aircraft could no longer land on the airfield for fear of being severely damaged by the Chinese.

During the whole battle, the artillery fired more than 2700 rounds but could not fire a single one in support of Rezang La.

He Escaped Chinese Captivity

Sep Nihal Singh, who was taken as a prisoner of war by the Chinese, was still in captivity in some Chinese camps. He remembers how he was taken prisoner by the Chinese after he got hit in the arms. He was asked his name several times, but he just said no. He was taken to a camp where he was offered some biscuits, but he refused to eat the enemy's food. He further says all the Chinese soldiers were enjoying themselves and drinking while he was partly unconscious. He could see two guards outside his tent. When they went away from his tent, he snuck out. He crossed the boundary of the camp, going in an unknown direction. When the Chinese got to know about his absence, they fired very loudly. He got frightened, thinking he might get caught again, but he kept walking, holding his left arm with his right hand. En route, he found a dog, which they used to call Tommy, that belonged to Tsaka-La Village. The soldiers of the company used to feed the dog while on Rezang La. The dog led the way, and Sep Nihal Singh followed. Following the dog for a few hours, he reached the battalion headquarters at night, where he was recognised by the soldiers and given treatment.

On the evening of November 19, troops from the 114th Brigade began to retreat from their positions, and by first light, all units had established depth positions in allotted locations. Tsaka La Company retreated to Dungti to join the 70 Infantry Brigade. Except for two RCL guns and two tanks that were damaged during the bombardment, all equipment was shifted. On November 21, the Chinese announced a cease-fire. Afterwards, the whole brigade withdrew, and a vehicle convoy with supplies and weaponry was dispatched to Leh. The Brigade suffered 140 fatalities of all ranks in the Battle of Chushul, compared to 1000+ casualties at the Chinese end.

References

1. Interview with Mr Narpat Singh
2. Interview with Commandant Prithvi Singh (retd)
3. Interview with Brigadier Raghunath V. Jatar (retd)
4. Interview with Brigadier Prem Kumar (retd)
5. Interview with Honorary Captain Ram Chander, 13 Kumaon (retd)
6. Interview with Havildar Nihal Singh, 13 Kumaon (retd)
7. Interview with Subedar Balwant Singh, 5 Jat (retd)
8. Telephonic Interview with Mrs Sheela Lamba w/o Brig B.S. Lamba
9. Telephonic Interview with Mrs Rani Khanna w/o Maj Gen R.K. Khanna
10. Interview with Mrs Shobha Rani w/o Brig Prem Kumar
11. Telephonic Interview with Mrs Pradanya Wakhle w/o Maj P.M. Wakhle
12. Telephonic Interview with Mrs Promila Shikarwar d/o Lt Col Mukut Singh
13. Telephonic Interview with Lt Gen Ramesh Halgali (retd) s/o Maj G. Halgali
14. Interview with Mrs Sunita Mukherjee d/o Col HS Dhingra, AVSM
15. Interview with Major Haramrit Singh Dhingra (retd) s/o Col H.S. Dhingra, AVSM
16. Telephonic Interview with Havildar Asha Ram, 13 Kumaon (retd)
17. Telephonic Interview with Havildar Sahi Ram, 13 Kumaon (retd)

18. Letters of Major Shaitan Singh, PVC
19. Documents of Major Shaitan Singh, PVC
20. Telephonic Interview with Mr Sandeep Kang Grandson of Lt Gen Bikram Singh
21. Telephonic Interview with Brigadier K.S. Kang (retd)
22. Telephonic Interview with Brigadier S.S. Kler (retd)
23. Telephonic Interview with Ms Poornima Thapa d/o Lt Col D.S. Thapa, PVC
24. Telephonic Interview with Lt Col Prem Singh (retd)
25. Interview with Mr Devraj Singh s/o Lt Col Bakhtawar Singh
26. Interview with Mrs Mahendra Kanwar daughter-in-law of Lt Col Sangram Singh (retd)
27. Book: *Valour Triumphs: A History of the Kumaon Regiment* Hardcover by K.C. Praval
28. Book: *Lest we Forget* by Capt Amarinder Singh
29. Telephonic Interview with the late Brig Balbir Singh Sandhu, 20 Lancers (retd)
30. Telephonic Interview with Mrs Avinash Chand
31. Telephonic Interview with Mrs Deepashree Mohan sister of Major S.D. Goswami, MVC
32. A visit to Chushul
33. Telephonic conversation with Maj Gen P.L. Kher, VrC (retd)
34. Telephonic conversation with Maj Gen A.K. Dewan, VrC (retd)

❑

Aftermath

Rezang La Memorial at Chushul after renovation

"Slowly and sadly we laid him down,
From the field of his fame fresh and gory;
We carved not a line, and we raised not a stone,
But we left him alone with his glory!"

– Charles Wolfe

The very last letter from Maj Shaitan Singh arrived at home on November 20. Shaitan Singh's family was relieved to get the letter because they were totally unaware that he had been killed in battle two days earlier. In response to the letter they had received on the 20th, they responded in writing. Major Shaitan Singh's family had officially been informed on November 21 that he was either suspected to have been taken prisoner or missing in action, but there was no definite information.

"In Ladakh, more details are now available regarding the Rezang La post, which fell on November 18. All our troops at the post held their ground to the last and inflicted very heavy casualties on the Chinese aggressors. There were very few survivors. The commander was seriously wounded. While he was being evacuated by two other ranks, they came under heavy fire. To save the lives of two other ranks, the officer ordered them to leave him where he was. The post fell after several hours of grim fighting when it became impossible to hold the Chinese attack."

This was the first coverage of Rezang La by the Press Information Bureau on November 22.

The brigade received a retreat order following the Chushul fight. The brigade headquarters gradually made its way to Leh after initially retreating to Bikaner Ridge, and then Chushul Village the following day.

The Paramvir Chakra

In December, 13 Kumaon found itself in Tangste Sarai, which is located around 50 miles northwest of Chushul. Lt Col H.S. Dhingra had forwarded citations for awards being bestowed to the troops of Charlie Company. His recommendation for Maj Shaitan Singh was for the Paramvir Chakra.

The first six Vir Chakra recommendations were made for posthumous honours: Nk Gulab Singh, L/Nk Singh Ram, Jem Surja Ram, Nk Hukam Chand, NA Dharampal Dahiya, Jem Hariram Yadav. The two living soldiers recommended were Jem Ram Chander, and Nk Ram Kumar.

CHM Harphool Singh, Hav Jai Narain, Hav Phool Singh, and Sep Nihal Singh were recommended for the Sena Medal, the CHM being posthumously recommended.

Lt Col Hari Singh Dhingra's name was recommended for the Mahavir Chakra by the Brigade Commander for his exemplary military leadership. For his fearless leadership during the conflict, the Brigade Commander was nominated for the Mahavir Chakra.

A Mahavir Chakra citation was claimed to be sent for Major Shaitan Singh. At the divisional level, the award approved was Mahavir Chakra, although Lt Gen Bikram Singh, who was in command of the 15 Corps in Udhampur, was well aware of Major Shaitan Singh's acts of courage. He had the distinct pleasure of recommending the award of the Paramvir Chakra to Major Shaitan Singh, who certainly deserved it.

Though there was no news of Shaitan's current situation in recent reports, word of his bravery had travelled far and wide, even globally.

Shaitan received a letter from Maj C.P. Singh Chaudhari, one of his friends who was serving with the Indian contingent in the Congo, dated December 13, 1962, from Leopoldville.

My dear Shaitan Singh

It was indeed heartwarming to hear about your deeds against the yellow rats. I must congratulate you for having fought so gallantly. I am sure you will be rewarded accordingly. I hope by now you have recovered from your wounds.

When you are fit, please drop me a few lines giving me details of the action you took. The paper gave only general terms.

We all in the Congo are looking forward to an early repatriation. We hope for the best.

With best wishes
Yours sincerely
C.P.S. Chaudhari

The battalion less Chalie Company relocated further north to Durbuk the following month, in January.

On the eve of Republic Day, Mrs. Sugan Kanwar, the wife of Maj Shaitan Singh, got a telegram that included two pieces of news: one was actually something to be quite proud of, and the other contained some heartbreaking information.

The telegram read:

Dear Madam,

I have great pleasure in communicating to you the award given by the President of Param-Vir-Chakra in recognition of the meritorious and conscious valour displayed by Major Shaitan Singh on November 18, 1962, in Ladakh. Please accept the warm congratulations of the Ministry of Defence on this great distinction conferred on your husband for his immortal valour.

I do hope Major Shaitan Singh, who is now missing and is believed to be a prisoner of war, will soon be able to join you and enjoy the distinction conferred on him.

Yours sincerely

DEFENCE MINISTRY

January 25, 1963

For his valiant actions during the battle of Rezang La, Maj Shaitan Singh was honoured with the Paramvir Chakra. Along with him, four of his soldiers received the Sena Medal, while eight of his soldiers received the Vir Chakra. Lt Col H.S. Dhingra, who had been recommended for a Mahavir Chakra, received a VSM Class II instead. The Mahavir Chakra was awarded to Brig T.N. Raina, 2/Lt Shyamal Dev Goswami, who suffered frostbite and lost both his legs, and Nk Rabi Lal Thapa.

Sqn Ldr Chandan Singh of the IAF, Capt Ashwani Kumar Dewan of the 20 Lancers, Capt P.L. Kher, Sub Amar Bahadur Gurung of 1/8 GR, and TA Gurdip Singh of the 38 Field Battery were awarded the Vir Chakra.

The fact that so many heroic soldiers were honoured was an enormous honour for 13 Kumaon and the Kumaon Regiment, but it was also extremely saddening to learn that the Chinese had already begun releasing lists of POWs, and that just four names from Charlie Company could be found on those lists. The remaining 110 were unaccounted for.

They Were Found But Dead

When February arrived, the battalion was still stationed in Durbuk. In the first week of February 1963, a local Ladakhi shepherd travelled through the Rezang La terrain with a herd of his livestock. He was astounded by the incredible battle spectacle of warriors frozen to death but still clutching their wrecked weapons. Their firearms were mostly empty, with bulging barrels from repeated shooting. He went down to inform the nearest Army unit that was a few kilometres away, after witnessing this incredible act of bravery, which was frozen to death. The Army and the administration concentrated primarily on the news.

The first Indian party of the International Red Cross and the Indian Army with cine and still cameras from the Press Information Bureau ascended Rezang La a week later, on February 12, 1963. Brig T.N. Raina was in command of the search team, which also included Lt Col H.S. Dhingra, AVSM, Sub Maj Changdi Ram, Maj Girish Narayan Sinha, the Battalion 2-IC and a number of other officials, and soldiers from 13 Kumaon. Adjutant of 1 Jat (LI) Capt K.S. Kang specifically requested his CO to allow him to join the search mission. He was given permission to join the team. What the team experienced and witnessed when they reached the summit was unprecedented.

The bunkers and fortifications that the Chinese shelling had destroyed were actually visible. The bullets and splinters had just shredded the sandbags. Everywhere was covered in artillery shells and bullet fragments. The group was now able to see the soldiers' riddled bodies, which had been shot through with bullets or splinters. Their hands were still tightly gripping weapons.

Dharampal Dhaiya, a nursing assistant, held a morphine syringe and a bandage. He died while saving another soldier.

During the last strike, the company's headquarters took a significant amount of shelling. Its ballies shrank down to the size of matchsticks. Till this point, there had been no indication of Maj Shaitan Singh's corpse. No one had been shot in the back while escaping, despite the fact that the team had so far discovered more than fifty bodies that were all riddled with bullets, all of them were shot in the front. All of them died bravely while fighting. When Brig T.N. Raina saw this, he lost control and began crying. Hony Capt Ram Chander recalls the scene and claims that Brig Raina wept so hard that his prosthetic eye fell to the ground (Brig Raina was wounded during the Burma Campaign due to a grenade burst and lost his eye).

Sep Ram Chander, Maj Shaitan Singh's radio operator, assisted in finding his body close to where the two Havildars and Ram Chander last saw him. His hands still held an LMG with the trigger depressed, and his body was still supported by the boulder. Due to the bitter cold, his entire face had turned black, and the wild crows of Ladakh had feasted on his nose and eyes. Eight bullet holes were discovered in his body, predominantly in and around his left arm and abdomen.

Up to February 13th, 97 bodies, including Maj Shaitan Singh's, have been found. Because the grip of the hands on the weapons was so firm, it was impossible to remove them without severing the fingers on the bodies that had weapons in their hands.

Yaks and ponies that were hired from the locals were used to help carry the bodies down.

Mrs. Shaitan Singh's life was shattered by a telegram she received from the GOC of Delhi and Rajasthan on the same day, February 13, 1815 hours. It said:

Major Shaitan Singh's body to arrive in Palam on February 15, and his funeral may be attended at Delhi Cantonment on the same day.

In an hour, she received another telegram from Delhi, this time from the Indian Army Headquarters.

Reference to our telegram of November Stop deeply regretting to inform your husband that Major Shaitan Singh has now been reported killed in action. Stop, please.

Accept my sincere condolences.

These two telegrams wreaked havoc on the family. Everyone was shocked. Many people had gathered around. Narpat in Ajmer didn't get any clue about what was happening in the village.

The cremation of the deceased became a topic of concern in Chushul. It was challenging to find wood for cremations in accordance with Hindu traditions because Ladakh was only a chilling desert with practically no vegetation. The men searched till they came across a school that was getting rid of its old furniture. That furniture was transported to the location where 13 Kumaon's Battalion HQs was located during the war. In presence of all the officers from 13 Kumaon, Maj Shaitan Singh's lifeless remains were given a guard of honour on February 15 and were then transported to Fukche Airfield. At the airfield was present a school friend, Maj Rewat Singh who was commanding a company of 9 Dogra. With a heavy heart he received the mortals of his friend with whom he spent his childhood days. Now a national hero but not present in this world. Giving a shoulder to his coffin was certainly not easy for him.

All 96 of the fallen soldiers in Chushul received a guard of honour in recognition of their valour. There was a huge funeral pyre arranged for mass cremation. With a heavy heart, Brig T.N. Raina lit the first pyre. Sub Hari Singh of 13 Kumaon who was unable to cope with the anguish and couldn't bear the pain of seeing so many dead comrades also passed away the prior evening due to a shock. He received the honours of being cremated alongside his 96 fellow soldiers. Twenty-six soldiers' bodies were discovered in the Gurung Hill region, and they were also cremated nearby at Chushul.

Jodhpur, One Last Time

The mortal remains of Maj Shaitan Singh were to be transported from Fukche to Delhi, where the cremation was scheduled to take place, in a special coffin packed with ice and placed in a transport aircraft of No. 19 TPT Squadron.

The Major's family had travelled from the village to Jodhpur. The family met Col Mohan Singh, who began getting in contact with people he knew in the military to find a way to transport Shaitan's lifeless remains to Jodhpur. Lt Gen Bikram Singh received a message in this regard. He reacted favourably to it. He gave the order to transport the mortal remains to Jodhpur.

The same aircraft which was to take off for Delhi departed on February 18; it was headed to Jodhpur this time. It was transporting the remains of Major Shaitan Singh, PVC, CO 13 Kumaon and a few Indian Air Force personnel.

At 15:42, the aircraft touched down at Jodhpur Airfield. To witness the valiant hero's dead body, a crowd had assembled. In the presence of Mohanlal Sukhadia, the Chief Minister of Rajasthan, the GOC Delhi and Rajasthan area received the body. Army and Air Force officers carried the casket on their shoulders.

At the airfield, 175 troops honoured the Paramvir with a guard of honour.

The casket was transported to Colonel Mohan Singh's home. Shaitan's body was to be brought to his house, not to the village, as he had demanded. He made a speech when receiving the body at his home with his eyes filled with tears. I was his commanding officer till this point, but from now on Shaitan Singh is my commanding officer.

Upon hearing of his father's passing, Narpat—who had also been called from Ajmer—arrived in Jodhpur. Upon seeing the body, which was covered in a white cloth, he simply hugged him and broke down in tears. The rites started later, and thousands of people gathered outside the house as the body was brought outside.

Major Shaitan Singh, PVC, began his final journey in Jodhpur. The procession's path spanned a distance of five miles. Thousands of people were chanting while standing on either side of the road. The Major's mortal remains were placed in the leading jeep as the procession left the Circuit House. The Rajasthan Armed Constabulary provided a guard of honour as the procession passed through Sojati Gate. The casket was taken out from the vehicle 500 yards from the Caga Crematorium. Soldiers carried the casket. A band of Jammu and Kashmir Rifles performed the last post on bugles and drums. The men marched firmly and slowly while carrying the coffin to Caga. On a platform the coffin was placed where wreaths were to be laid.

Wreaths were laid on behalf of the President, Prime Minister, Governor of Rajasthan, Defence Minister, GOC-in-C Western Command, Colonel of the Kumaon Regiment, and some royal families of Rajasthan.

After the wreath-laying ceremony the body was taken out of the coffin to be put on the funeral pyre. The last rituals commenced when Narpat lit his father's pyre, exactly three months after his death at the battle of Rezang La.

Hundreds of journalists covered this topic over the next few days. There were coming accounts of awe and thankfulness from all throughout the nation. In commemoration of the legendary Maj Shaitan Singh, PVC, some mothers even gave their children the name Shaitan Singh.

In May 1963, Maj Dhan Singh Thapa with 5 Jat, and 13 Kumaon POWs were all returned back to India. These battalions had previously changed locations around Tangste and Durbuk. Five PoWs of 13 Kumaon came back including Jem Ram Chander, VrC and Sepoy Ram Singh who had lost both his legs due to wounds. He was amputated in enemy captivity.

Rezang La Memorial

In honour of their slain comrades, 13 Kumaon had begun construction on a memorial at the cremation site. On August 5, 1963, the rising day of 13 Kumaon, Lt Col Hari Singh Dhingra, AVSM, formally inaugurated the memorial. Col Dhingra, who was a student of English literature himself chose the lines to be engraved on the memorial's pillar which still inspires the generations;

"And how can man die better
than facing fearful odds,
for the ashes of his fathers,
and the temples of his Gods?"

— Thomas Babington Macaulay

The other memorial was built close to Chushul Village to remember the brave Gorkhas and Gunners.

In tribute to the valiant son of the soil, Major Shaitan Singh's hometown of Banasar was renamed Shaitan Singh Nagar in August 1963. Even now, houses in the area still display pictures of Maj Shaitan Singh in their homes.

The royal family of Jodhpur and the Chief Minister of Rajasthan were among the dignitaries who paid their respects to the family and the slain hero during their visits. The Jaipur Darbar also presented Tazim to Major Shaitan Singh. Numerous military officers wrote letters of sympathy. But Shaitan's family remains heartbroken over his tragic death.

The family was brought to Delhi in January 1964, two days before Republic Day. There they met Maj Dhan Singh Thapa and Mrs. Joginder Singh, who had all travelled to get their Paramvir Chakras.

Mrs. Shaitan Singh was presented with the Paramvir Chakra and the citation in honour of her brave husband on January 26, 1963.

The citation read:

Major Shaitan Singh was commanding a company of an infantry battalion deployed at Rezang La in the Chusul sector at a height of about 17,000 feet. The locality was isolated from the main defence sector and consisted of five platoon-defended positions. On November 18, 1962, the Chinese forces subjected the company position to heavy artillery, mortar, and small arms fire and attacked it with overwhelming strength in several successive waves. Against heavy odds, our troops beat back successive waves of enemy attack. During the action, Major Shaitan Singh dominated the scene of operations and moved at great personal risk from one platoon post to another, sustaining the morale of his hard-pressed platoon posts. While doing so, he was seriously wounded but continued to encourage and lead his men, who, following his brave example, fought gallantly and inflicted heavy casualties on the enemy. For every man lost to us, the enemy lost four or five. When Major Shaitan Singh fell disabled by wounds in his arms and abdomen, his men tried to evacuate him, but they came under heavy machine-gun fire. Major Shaitan Singh then ordered his men to leave him to his fate in order to save their lives.

Major Shaitan Singh's supreme courage, leadership, and exemplary devotion to duty inspired his company to fight almost to the last man.

The loss of Shaitan was undoubtedly a devastating blow to the family. The strongest support system for the family was gone. Regaining stability took a long time. Narpat had stopped studying. Mrs. Shaitan's health began to deteriorate, and she stopped going out of her home. Mr Narpat Singh was married to Ms Usha Kanwar who is the daughter of Mr Khet Singh Rathore a reputed politician, former Home Minister of Rajasthan and a childhood friend of Maj Shaitan Singh. The couple was blessed with three daughters Kiran Singh, Rashmi Singh and Rithu Singh. The family resides in Jodhpur.

PVC Handed Over To 13 Kumaon

Following the successful campaign against Pakistan in 1971, Lt Col R.V. Jatar's 13 Kumaon arrived in Jodhpur in 1972. Some officers and soldiers of the battalion travelled from Jodhpur to Shaitan Singh Nagar to pay respects to Maj Shaitan Singh's family. The bust of Major Shaitan Singh was erected in the battalion that same year on Rezang La Day, or November 18, in the presence of his son. Additionally, Narpat Singh presented 13 Kumaon with his father's Paramvir Chakra. The medal was received by Lt Col R.V. Jatar on behalf of 13 Kumaon.

Memorials

A memorial at the cremation site was also erected by Maj Shaitan Singh's son, in commemoration of the funeral day of his father.

In 1992, GOC 12 Division Maj Gen G.C. Bhandari, a part of the 20th Rajput (Jodhpur), a unit Shaitan had previously served with as a subaltern, to commemorate the thirty years anniversary of the Battle of Rezang La. The bust of Mrs. Sugan Kanwar's husband had been installed at a well-known circle in Jodhpur city, and Gen Bhandari had invited her to unveil it. This was the only event Mrs. Shaitan had ever attended, despite the fact that numerous memorials and places were named in honour of Maj Shaitan Singh. With pride in her heart and tears in her eyes, she unveiled the bust.

On the occasion of the 50th anniversary of the conflict, Mr. Narpat Singh was formally invited to Rezang La in 2012. He travelled to Rezang La for the first time in 50 years.

Mrs. Sugan Kanwar, who was separated from her husband for fifty years, finally reunited with him again on April 17, 2015. Military honours were performed during her funeral. Despite the fact that she never stayed with him during any tenure. I believe they are both now blissfully residing in the afterlife.

A unit of the Kumaon Regiment erected a memorial in 2020 during Snow Leopard at the exact spot where Maj Shaitan Singh was reportedly mortally wounded. The old Rezang La Memorial, which had undergone a few renovations, was to receive a makeover that year, according to an order given by India's defence minister. The task of renovating the memorial fell to the Northern Army Command. The memorial was exquisitely constructed and designed. Shri Rajnath Singh, India's defence minister, officially inaugurated it on November 18, 2021, in the presence of CDS Gen Bipin Rawat, Brig Raghunath V. Jatar (retd.) Mr. Narpat Singh, Mrs. Sunita Mukherjee, Maj Haramrit Singh Dhingra (retd.), as well as a number of other dignitaries and military officials. I had the good fortune to be present for the ceremony and visit the Rezang La Memorial on its opening day.

Maj Shaitan Singh, PVC, left behind a legacy that would inspire generations to come. People in the nation would never forget his brave actions.

"Unka naam Shaitan tha, par vo Bhagwan they."

–A soldier who had served with him

References

1. Interview with Mr Narpat Singh
2. Interview with Commandant Prithvi Singh (retd)
3. Interview with Mr Mahendra Singh s/o Mr Mool Singh
4. Interview with Mr Manvendra Singh Grandnephew of Major Shaitan Singh, PVC
5. Interview with Brig Raghunath V. Jatar (retd)
6. Telephonic Interview with Mrs Pradanya Wakhle w/o Maj P.M. Wakhle (retd)
7. Interview with Major Haramrit Singh Dhingra (retd) s/o Col H.S. Dhingra, AVSM (retd)
8. Telephonic Interview with Brig K.S. Kang (retd)
9. Interview with Advocate Naresh Chouhan
10. A visit to Chushul

❑

Epilogue

"...For he who sheds his blood with me today, shall remain my brother forever!"

–William Shakespeare

Why do men fight and give up their life in wars? What compels them to disregard the biological procedure of self-preservation and stand beside each other to the end? What was so special about the company at Rezang La that it fought to the last man on those icy deserted mountain pass?

As a civilian myself, I have grappled with this question for too long and depiction of battle in the Indian popular culture has never been able to satisfy my curiosity on the subject. During the course of my research, perhaps I was able to get certain insights into this psychology of brotherhood bound together. Most importantly by immediate leadership which instils trust and confidence amongst men to achieve something extraordinary and to extract unflinching loyalty and following.

As I delved deeper into the life of Maj Shaitan Singh, PVC. I learnt something unconventional and unique about leadership. Something which was against my well established idea of behavioural traits exuded by great military leaders.

The most prevalent perception of leadership or a military leader is that they are bold, strongly built, and possessed of a certain level of professional arrogance. But this isn't always the case; some people have short or medium heights, gentle voices, and very kind personalities. The trait we consistently overlook in a leader is the way he behaves. I discovered that behaviour is a crucial aspect of military leadership. It goes without saying that a leader needs to feel a strong connection to individuals he is commanding.

I conducted a thorough life study of Major Shaitan Singh in order to identify all the facets of his character that were demonstrated on the battlefield and that were intricately linked to various junctures in his personal and professional development. I'd like to explain a few of them to the readers.

The first people that come to mind when we hear the phrase "military leadership" are often from the West and have received military leadership and training along Western standards. But in this case, we discover a man who received his training using British-derived Indian training methods. A brief look back at this book reveals a father who moved through the ranks to become a senior commander, and his son, who was expected to join the military, is uninterested in doing so. What led him to believe he had enlisted in the state force is very unclear. I immediately observed the first trait in him which is his unpredictable nature but this similar characteristic cannot be seen in his leadership.

A common practice in state forces during training was to instil in the cadets the motto "Either you win or die" and there is no place for defeat in a warrior's life they are made to achieve the objective and if not successful in doing so they readily embrace death with both hands. This was done in order to mentally prepare them for the approaching events or operations. Maj Shaitan Singh did the same thing; he preferred death to defeat.

Fortunately, I was able to communicate with one of his superiors from the Kotah Umed Infantry. A few days ago, he died. He explained to me that although Shaitan was popular and well-liked by fellow soldiers, the CO had to reprimand him early on since he lacked certain abilities. The question that follows is: What do your men appreciate that your superior does not?

The answer is simple: people behave differently when they are in positions of authority versus when they are not. It gives a strong indication of personality. Some people are adept at demonstrating their qualities, while others are not as capable at doing so to higher authorities. But they all possess and use these qualities when they are in positions of authority. His men must have adored him for being an honest person at heart but superiors who are experienced expect one to grow professionally too.

The impact of his superiors on his life was something else I had noticed. His father, a decorated officer, must have had a direct or indirect impact on his personality as he developed as a leader. Then his superiors and commanding officers arrive. Even serving alongside some of them may have increased Shaitan Singh's desire to fight for the motherland. Officers like Lt Col Jaswant Sinh, MBE, Lt Col Kaman Singh, MVC, or Lt Gen Bikram Singh, who were all war veterans and highly decorated officers with high leadership acumen, had all indirectly influenced Shaitan Singh's mindset at different stages of his career.

Similarly, when we read a letter from him to his friend 'Maj Mal Singh, it states: Mal ji, you got a chance to fight, and I did absolutely nothing here'. It shows and points out his will to do something for the country.

The most significant aspect of his personality that I have observed is his extremely kind and modest demeanour. After speaking to more than ten people who knew him personally or served alongside him, I came to a conclusion. His considerate behaviour helped him gain his soldiers' respect. Due to his temperament, he won the affection of everyone wherever he went. He stood out from other people because of this. No one has ever alleged that Maj Shaitan Singh has ever acted rudely or brutally in the interviews I've conducted. He always had a very calm, compassionate and gentle disposition towards his family, friends, and soldiers.

Major Sahab used to treat us all like family, according to one of the soldiers who survived through the war. He never yelled at us, frequently inquired about the welfare of our families, and showed concern for us. He never boasted about his ranks by claiming to be a captain or a major. He was an extremely gracious individual. This suggests that the company commander and the soldiers who followed him got along well. This was one of the factors that made his troops on the battlefield absolutely prepared to kill or be killed at his command.

Knowledge and experience have an essential role in leadership. As is well known, during the war, the 13 Kumaon Regiment had been posted in eastern Ladakh. High-altitude mountains in Ladakh experience harsh winter weather. If Shaitan Singh were to be examined in this situation, I would see a very appropriate man in charge of the troops. We can see from his career that he served in Dras with the Kotah Umed Infantry. Being the second-coldest inhabited region in the world, he had encountered both the weather and the high-altitude terrain. In addition, he had served in Dras just as the first Indo-Pak War was coming to an end. So it is clear that he had a degree of familiarity with mountain combat strategies. He led his men better at Rezang La as he had had these specific leadership experiences. I strongly believe if he had not possessed this experience, he would certainly have faced more difficulties.

The second point is that more than half his career was spent in the field, where he participated in the preparation and execution of operations, first in Dras and then twice in Naga Hills, once with 6 Kumaon and another time with 23 Infantry Division. As a result, I think he possessed both a strategic and executional attitude.

The usage of mortars during the Battle of Rezang La is one significant aspect that stands out. If we examine Maj Shaitan Singh's career, we can see that he completed the 3-inch mortar training and held the position of mortar platoon commander for an extended period of time. At Rezang La, the choice of the killing area and the defence fire were both excellent. Given the volume of ammunition used during the war, mortars must have caused enormous damage. This is a prime instance of applying his expertise from leading a mortar platoon.

I conclude my remarks on his leadership with an adequately balanced account. Shaitan Singh impresses me as a very kind person who was a competent leader but also unpredictable. At every level of his professional life, he had become better. He was incredibly resourceful and had a strong sense of responsibility. He gained the respect of his colleagues by using his interpersonal skills, which enabled him to extract the best possible performance out of them. Instead of always being the bold and flamboyant leader who leads the hardest battles. I believe that quiet and compassionate commanders sometimes have the uncanny capacity and confidence to alter the course of the war.

I finish my narrative with an important message from a soldier:

A battlefield requires nerves of steel from a commander. I was told when I was a young officer by a brigadier that if a company commander has to use his weapon to make a difference on the battlefield, he has already lost the battle. He has to be seen standing tall, encouraging men to fight, disregarding his personal safety, not coming under pressure, and using calculated wits to always remain in control.

The same thing happened to Maj Shaitan Singh on the battlefield; he stood upright, led his soldiers to stop the enemy, and, disregarding his own safety, went head-to-head with death.

As a result, he gained the reputation of being one of the renowned military leaders, whose bravery and abilities are even disparaged by the enemy.

Leadership is not for recognition but to extract and perform. A humble, honest and dedicated person can be as effective a leader than our conventional hard taskmaster and flamboyant leaders both in military and corporates.

❑

End Note

Author at Rezang La Memorial on the day of inauguration

"Those who are prepared to die for any cause are seldom defeated."

–Pandit Jawarharlal Nehru

I was a college student in 2018 when I first heard about Major Shaitan Singh, PVC. In January 2019, while travelling, I came across a video that told the story of the battle of Rezang La. In the story, a survivor of the battle said, "Unka naam Shaitan tha, par vo Bhagwan theh." That particular line stuck in my mind. I wondered if he fought such a terrific battle that he must have an aggressive personality. But according to this survivor, he was completely the opposite. This made me curious to find out more about him.

On February 2, 2019, I took part in a college story-telling competition. I told a true account of a tough battle while everyone else was talking about fictitious stuff. However, I came in at the bottom spot. Maybe it's because my story wasn't fascinating or maybe it's because no one understood the premise of it. I may have lost the competition that day, but I gained something more significant. I became curious about why I lost. I was interested in learning more about the conflict and the person. I set out to look for his family. I was unable to find anything online. I contacted various organisations, but they all responded negatively. After speaking to Sainik Kalyan Vibhag Jodhpur, I was able to obtain his son's address. I found it on Google Maps and received his son's contact details. I got in touch with him in July, and it took me till November 26, four more months, to see him. I made the crucial decision to pen this biography of Major Shaitan Singh, PVC. I, a novice writer, initially believed that I would finish this book in a short period of time. I did begin writing, but I wasn't happy with the information I had gathered. I wanted more. I had some challenges as well. I started getting in touch with Maj Shaitan Singh's family members, friends, and the families of his friends. When I was having one such conversation, the daughter of Lt Col Dhan Singh Thapa, PVC, asked me to go to Chushul once, but it seemed absolutely impossible for me to do so.

In the year 2021, I began interacting with others. Till the month of June, when I got an inquiry from an officer asking for some information about Major Shaitan Singh, PVC, who was in charge of renovating the Rezang La Memorial at Chushul, I had amassed a sizeable amount of data and images. It was an honour for me to give the Army photos and information. My research went on. When November arrived, I had no plans to travel to Ladakh till November 8 when the officer sent me a photograph of a design in which I could see my name written,

"The information and pictures in this section are courtesy of Mr. Jai Samota."

It was a moment of pride for me and my family. I asked the officer if I could attend the inauguration ceremony held on the 18th, or Rezang La Day. He immediately replied, Yes.

On the 13th, I found myself on a flight to Leh with Brigadier Raghunath V. Jatar and his grandson. After landing in Leh, he took me with him to his guest room, where I stayed for four days before going to Chushul. The ceremony was to be attended by Mr. Narpat Singh and his son-in-law, Mrs. Sunita Mukherjee, and Major Haramrit Singh Dhingra.

On the 17th, Mr. Narpat Singh's son-in-law and I travelled by road from Leh to reach Tangste. En route we stopped at Zingral, which is located at a height of 15000 feet. There, I experienced slight breathing difficulties. I had a physical examination, and everything seemed fine. Once again on the go, we made a halt at Chang-La. Breathing became harder and harder for me. I checked myself again, and things were worse this time. I had a 53 per cent SpO2 level. When I saw the numbers, I was stunned. I was asked to descend to a lower altitude after receiving oxygen for 30 minutes. At Tsolak Medical Post, we stopped before resuming our journey. High-altitude illness was diagnosed with me. My oxygen saturation has risen to 66 per cent. I received saline, oxygen, and medications. We were asked to move to Tangste after I started to feel better. I was relieved to be so near Rezang La when I arrived at Tangste around 1400 hours, which served as our night halt. But this was untrue. A nursing assistant arrived to see how I was feeling. He observed how much my oxygen levels were fluctuating. He requested an ambulance, and it arrived to transport me to Field Hospital. where a doctor came to check on me. She checked my blood pressure first, which was normal. She then checked my heart rate, which was the worrying part. Approximately 170. To screen for high-altitude pulmonary edema, she performed a few procedures, including an ECG and an X-ray. I was given admission to an ICU. Fortunately, I was safe. But she refused to allow me to travel further. She asked me to return to Leh before heading back home. The hospital's commanding officer, who visited me in the evening, said the same thing to me. Although I was quite disappointed to hear that, I didn't give up hope. I told my family about the incident, but I didn't make clear how terrible it was. Hearing all this had already made them anxious. I was certain that I was going to attend because I had spoken to various officers till this point. My health had significantly improved when I woke up in the morning at 0500 hours. However, when I got in touch with my liaison officer, he said that because I was being taken to Leh, he had been told to leave me at the hospital and continue. I learned that the ambulance had also left for Leh 15 minutes prior. I was now stuck at the hospital. My chances of getting to Chushul were dwindling. I received a call from the officer who had allowed me to travel to Ladakh, telling me not to go if I wasn't feeling well. Sir, even if I'm going to die, I'll come to Rezang La, I replied in Josh.

I unexpectedly got a call from a different officer who was handling the travel arrangements. He told me that instead of transporting me to Chushul, he had scheduled another ambulance to take me to Leh. I was so close to Rezang La; I was shattered. By this time, my hope was gone. My family was sad when I told them. They began to pray. I prayed sincerely; someone must have heard my prayers, since fifteen minutes later the same officer called. He said, "Jai, I've set up a vehicle with two oxygen cylinders." You'll be taken straight to the Rezang La Memorial. That day, I realised that miracles happen and that when you truly want something to happen, it will. After arriving at Rezang La Memorial, I went to the official inaugural event where the former CDS and the defence minister were present. I was questioned by a few people who wanted to know how I got to Rezang La after spending the night in the hospital. Where there is a will, there is a way, Brigadier Raghunath V. Jatar responded. My dream had indeed come true. All thanks to the officer who permitted me to visit and to my family due to whom I went to Rezang La.

I continued my research after returning from Ladakh in order to discover more. I was curious as to what had transformed Shaitan Singh into the well-known Major Shaitan Singh. I conducted interviews with several people I met. I visited every state in northern India, with the exception of two, in my search for the man. I got to know battle veterans and individuals who had seen him. I met his friends. People cried while talking about him, and I saw it. I encountered many ups and downs. Many people called my effort a waste of time and ridiculed it. Why did you decide to write on such a dated subject? I responded by saying, "I didn't pick a subject to write about." I had no desire to write a book when I went to his place. However, it was fate that prompted me to explore, look for, and write about this man, who we refer to as Major Shaitan Singh, PVC.

I spent four years of my life finding him. Now I can claim with pride that I got to meet the man who never intended to join the Fauj but fought the Battle of Rezang La. Yes he never liked his name, he tried to get it changed but couldn't. It was his destiny that his name Shaitan is now engraved in golden words of the nation's history and became one of the most acclaimed figures in the Indian Army. Certainly, I found him very competent, experienced, yet a shy person.

No one knows when the Major breathed his last. But as much as I know him, with every breath ebbing out, subtracting the last few seconds of his life, he certainly would have smiled a little and thought of his company, which put up such a fierce fight against the mighty enemy, and for sure he would have remembered the line that was told to him during his junior command that he lacked assertiveness in his leadership and needed to improve his self-confidence. The thought of his school teacher saying to him, "Ek din yeh bohot badi shaitani karega," would've crossed his mind.

The last thought that passed his mind before breathing the last would certainly be of his family—his wife and son, whom he wanted to celebrate Diwali with but couldn't.

After a challenging 1600-day journey, I finally added these final words in the biography of Major Shaitan Singh, PVC. It, obviously, redefined the trajectory of my life and absolutely transformed me as a person. With so many people, notably Major Shaitan Singh, who must be blessing us from above, I formed wonderful associations—both general and emotional.

This one's for you Shaitsa!

❑

Messages

"Shaitan Singh is not only the heroic symbol of Rajasthan but also of India. His sacrifice will always be inspirational. One who has a brave heart can fire a gun. A weak person cannot handle weapons and he can only harm himself out of cowardice."

–Yashwantrao Balwantrao Chavan
Defence Minister of India

"The valour displayed by Shaitan Singh of Rajasthan is heard by everyone. He has become a historical figure of Ladakh. He kept fighting even after he was shot in the arm. He fell only when a bullet hit him in the stomach. Inspired by his bravery, other soldiers of his company also fought with their lives at risk. A total of two or three persons returned from his company, the rest all attained martyrdom. Shaitan Singh refused to be taken down and expressed his desire that he should be allowed to die on the battlefield itself. The name of Rajasthan has been glorified by his glorious valour."

–Mohan Lal Sukhadia
Chief Minister Rajasthan

"When I first saw Shaitan Singh as a football player, I had guessed on the same day that this boy is promising. I asked him what career do you want to choose? So, he replied that he wanted to be a lawyer. I asked him not to become a lawyer and join the army, and he agreed. Then I recruited him as a cadet in my unit Durga Horse. From that day his military life started.

Till now I considered myself as his CO. But from January 26 our relationship has changed. Now Shaitan Singh is my CO. And I am his soldier."

–Colonel Mohan Singh
Jodhpur State Forces

"I write to express the deep sympathy and condolence of myself and all ranks in the Army on the sad and untimely death of your husband, Major Shaitan Singh. Your husband fought gallantly and made the supreme sacrifice for the sake of the Motherland, a noble death for any soldier.

I hope you will bear this loss with courage and fortitude with the knowledge that we share your sorrow."

–General J.N. Chaudhari
Chief of Army Staff

"I have great pleasure in communicating to you the award by the President of Param Vir Chakra in recognition of the most conspicuous gallantry displayed by Major Shaitan Singh on November 18, 1962 in Ladakh. Please accept the warmest congratulations of the Ministry of Defence on this great distinction conferred on your husband for his immortal valour. I do hope that Major Shaitan Singh, who is now missing and is believed to be a prisoner of war, will soon be able to join you and enjoy the distinction conferred on him."

–P.V.R. RAO
Defence Secretary

"I have learnt with deep regret of the news of Maj Shaitan Singh being missing in battle, though from all accounts I hear that the officer fought in the service of the country with great gallantry to the last moment.

I can well imagine the deep sorrow this would cause in the family, and my feeling and heartfelt sympathy is very much with you in this sad hour.

With my sincere and heartfelt sympathy in your sad hour."

–Lt Gen K. Bahadur Singh
Colonel of the Kumaon Regiment

"I am really proud that I had officers like the late Major Shaitan Singh under my command both here and in Naga Hills. I had the highest regard for him ever since I came in close touch with him and there was no doubt in my mind that he had all the qualities of a perfect gentleman and a brave soldier and that one day he was sure to make a name for himself and his family. Though Major Shaitan Singh is no more in this world, he has made himself immortal by his supreme sacrifice for the cause of our motherland. Needless to say that the future progeny will always remember with reverence people like Major Shaitan Singh who never hesitated to pay the highest price in keeping the hard won freedom of the country. I would like to congratulate you and the family for producing such an outstanding soldier. It is not only the Army but the whole country is indebted to him. It is not necessary for me to say anything further. There are the words and there are the deeds and by his action Major Shaitan Singh has certainly become a martyr."

–Lt Gen Bikram Singh

"You rarely come across such examples in the annals of world military history when braving such heavy odds, the men fought till the last bullet and the last man. Certainly, the battle of Rezang La is such a shining example."

–Brigadier (later General) T.N. Raina
114 Brigade Commander

"Due to the extraordinary bravery, courage and efficient leadership shown by Major Shaitan Singh, the Government of India has conferred the award of 'Param Vir Chakra' (posthumously) on him. On this occasion, I and the Officers, JCOs and the soldiers of my paltan heartily congratulate you.

This deed of his has not only increased the prestige of our Paltan, but has also raised the pride and honour of the entire army and the country, it will be an ideal example for the generations to come."

–Lieutenant Colonel H.S. Dhingra, AVSM
CO 13 Kumaon

"Shaitan Singh, I saw him as a second lieutenant, young officer and obedient. He used to carry out senior officers' orders very obediently. But for me to judge his potential capabilities in an operation was too early."

–Major Bakhtawar Singh Brar (retd)
Senior of Maj Shaitan Singh in 6 Kumaon

"Major Shaitan Singh was son of Lt Col Thakur Hem Singh, OBI. He completed his education from Rajput School, Chopasni and Jaswant College.

Originally he started his military career from Durga Horse, Jodhpur. After commissioning he was posted to Kotah Umed Infantry. He joined the unit in Dras, after the Indo-Pak War of 1948. He was a very brave leader of whom his men were proud of. His men appreciated his bravery."

–Colonel Shivji Singh (retd)
Senior of Maj Shaitan Singh in Kotah Umed Infantry

"It is rare to find a young man of 21 years with so much knowledge of military and general affairs. Jai is an observant man with good memories. With determination he successfully managed to come to Chushul for the crucial renovation function, though some authorities were reluctant.

I wish him great success as a Military Historian."

–Brigadier Raghunath V. Jatar (retd)
Colleague of Maj Shaitan Singh, PVC

"Major Shaitan Singh was being evacuated by two Other Ranks the party came under heavy machine gun fire. To save the lives of the two jawans Major Shaitan Singh ordered them to leave him and look after themselves. 'Leave me here, save yourself. This is an order', this is what Major Shaitan Singh told his men who were carrying him away to safety from the Rezang La post. The two other ranks carried him some distance and laid the gallant Company Commander down next to a boulder on the slopes of the hill. They hoped for the best.

Major Shaitan Singh had spoken feebly. With a faint smile and with his eyes dropping, he bade his faithful comrades farewell. He held on to his stomach which had been torn open. Blood gushed out of the fatal wound. His arms had little strength. They lost their grip and then hung limp.

The body of Major Shaitan Singh was found exactly where it had been placed by his jawans. It was brought from there and flown to Jodhpur where it was cremated with full military honours....

For his 'supreme courage, leadership and exemplary devotion to duty (which) inspired his Company to fight gallantly almost to the last man', Major Shaitan Singh was awarded the Param Vir Chakra posthumously."

–Lt Gen D.D. Saklani (retd)
Junior of Maj Shaitan Singh

"He was older than all of us. Sometimes, if a junior showed up late for lunch or supper, he would wait for him before beginning his meal. He never argued with anyone or demanded to know why he was late. He used to join us for every supper. He never spoke to us as his juniors. Rather, he always regarded us like younger brothers."

Great honour to meet Jai. Thank you God almighty for your kindness.

God bless Jai!"

–Brigadier Prem Kumar (retd)
Junior of Maj Shaitan Singh

"A pleasure to meet an eminent historian who has been exploring the history of the Indian Army during the 1962 war. As I took an active part in this war in the Chushul sector in Ladakh. It will be my privilege to share a few events of the war with you, while I was posted with 1 Jat (LI).

Wish you all the best for your endeavour of doing a noble cause.

All the best."

–Colonel S.P. Dua (retd)
QM 1 Jat (LI) counterpart of Maj Shaitan Singh before the war.

"My husband Brig B.S. Lamba was commissioned in 13 Kumaon in June 1957. We were married on 4th December 1961. Our first station after marriage was Ambala. 13 Kumaon had returned after liberating Goa. Every day celebrations were going on. That's where I met Major Shaitan Singh. What I recollect is that he was a simple, unassuming and a thorough gentleman. My husband had tremendous regard for him; he was like an elder brother to him, always guiding him and other young officers. Major Shaitan Singh the hero of the battle of Chushul will be remembered forever."

–Mrs Sheela Lamba
w/o Brig B.S. Lamba

"I'm the daughter of Colonel Mukut Singh who commanded 13 Kumaon Regiment. All I remember about Major Shaitan Singh uncle is; he was a Brave Army Officer who fought the 1962 War and sacrificed his life while fighting bravely. He was awarded the Param Vir Chakra Award and we are proud of knowing and having Major Shaitan Singh in the 13 Kumaon Battalion."

–Mrs Promila Soam
d/o Lt Col Mukut Singh

"Mr Jai Samota has very painstakingly written this excellent biography of his hero Major Shaitan Singh, PVC. He delved deep into every stage of the life of his hero.

An extremely well researched book, it brings out several aspects hitherto unknown. Jai made several ground visits to various places where Maj Shaitan Singh served. He interviewed many erstwhile colleagues of Maj Shaitan Singh, and also his surviving family members in Rajasthan.

He also brings out Major Shaitan Singh's initial service in Jodhpur State Forces post Second World War till 1949 when he moved to Dras as part of Kotah Infantry. My father late Lt Col Madho Singh also served in Jodhpur State infantry in the Second World War and till 1951 when he was transferred to 3 Gorkha Rifles.

With remarkable passion Mr Jai Samota endeavoured to ensure no gaps are left in narrating the life and actions of Major Shaitan Singh, whether in the Battle of Rezang La or elsewhere.

From the efforts of Jai Samota, a biography of infinite value has emerged, befitting the illustrious image of the indomitable Major Shaitan Singh, PVC."

–Lt Gen N.K. Singh, PVSM, UYSM, AVSM, VSM (retd)
Former Deputy Chief, Indian Army

❑

Appendix- I

Survivors of the Battle

1. Jemadar Ram Chander Yadav, VrC (later Honorary Captain)
2. Naik Ram Kumar Yadav, VrC (later Honorary Captain)
3. Naik Bhay Ram Yadav
4. Sepoy Phool Singh Yadav, SM (later Honorary Captain)
5. Sepoy Nihal Singh Yadav, SM (later Havildar)
6. Sepoy Jai Narain Yadav, M-in-D (later Naib Subedar)
7. Sepoy Jai Narain Yadav (later Naib Subedar)
8. Sepoy Mam Chand Yadav
9. Sepoy Jaswant Singh Yadav
10. Sepoy Asha Ram Yadav (later Honorary Captain)
11. Sepoy Ram Chander Yadav (later Honorary Captain)
12. Sepoy Gaje Singh Yadav (later Havildar)
13. Sepoy Ram Singh Yadav
14. Sepoy Ram Nath Yadav (later Honorary Captain)
15. Sepoy Mithai Lal
16. Sepoy Jai Ram Yadav (Cook)
17. Sepoy Ramdhari (Washerman)

Appendix - II

List of names of officers who served with Major Shaitan Singh,PVC and are mentioned in this book.

1. Lieutenant Colonel Hem Singh, OBI retired in 1935. He was re-employed as a liaison officer during the second world war. He passed away in May 1951.

Durga Horse

1. Colonel Mohan Singh stayed in service of Jodhpur; he never joined the Indian Army.
2. SOC Hari Singh went to JSI after independence and later to 4/9 Gorkha Rifles and he retired as a Brigadier and earned an AVSM.
3. SOC Durga Das was transferred to the 63rd Cavalry and he became a Major before retiring.

Kotah Umed Infantry

1. Lieutenant Colonel Durjan Sal Singh retired from the same rank and he commanded Kota Sub Sector, Mewar Bhil Corps, 3 Bihar and 1 Assam Rifles before retiring.
2. Lieutenant Colonel Jaswant Sinh Parmar, MBE remained as the last CO of Kotah Umed Infantry and became the first CO of Mewar Infantry (Rajputana Rifles) he also commanded 17 Rajput and an NCC Battalion before retiring.
3. Major Sangram Singh participated in the 1962 war as a company commander of 5 Jat and he raised 7 Jat and

also commanded 18 Assam Rifles. He remained Deputy Commandant of Jat Regimental Centre and he retired as a Lt Col.

4. Major Bhairon Singh participated in the 1962 war as a company commander of 5 Jat and he went on to command 11 Jat.
5. Major Gulab Singh was transferred to 13 Kumaon and he retired as a Major from military police.
6. Major Veer Singh was transferred to the Jat Regiment.
7. Major Shivji Singh retired as a Colonel, he commanded 3 Grenadiers and later the Grenadiers Regimental Centre. He died on June 11, 2023.
8. Captain Pratap Singh went on to become a Major and was transferred to the Assam Regiment.
9. Captain Himmat Singh Rajvi went on to become a Major and he died in 2019 at the age of 107.

Jodhpur Sardar Infantry

1. Lieutenant Colonel Dhonkal Singh went on to command 3 Dogra and retired from the same rank.
2. Captain Chandan Singh went to the Indian Air Force and he participated in 1962, 1965 and 1971 wars which earned him MVC, an AVSM and a VrC he retired as an Air Vice Marshal.
3. Lieutenant Rewat Singh remained with JSI/20 Rajput and commanded the same. He retired as a Colonel.
4. Lieutenant Rewat Singh of Dhaka participated in the 1962 war as a company commander. He went on to become a Lt Col and he commanded 9 Dogra.
5. Lieutenant Mal Singh went on to become a Lt Col and he was awarded Shaurya Chakra Class III.

6. Lieutenant Mod Singh retired as a Major.
7. Lieutenant Moti Singh retired as a Major.
8. Second Lieutenant Bijai Singh was transferred to 22 Punjab and later he went to command 13 Grenadiers in the 1971 War before retiring from Military Police.

6 Kumaon

1. Lieutenant Colonel Kaman Singh, MVC went on to command 6 Assam Rifles and later 3 Kumaon Rifles and he died while on active duty in July 1956.
2. Lt Col H.S. Virk, MVC, DSO commanded 6 Kumaon till Feb 1955.
3. Major H.S. Bolina, VrC went on to become a Brigadier.
4. Major Prem H. Honawar went on to become a Major General.
5. Captain Bakhtawar Singh Brar went on to become a Major. After retirement he moved to the USA where he started farming. He happily lives in California and is currently aged 109 years.
6. Captain C.N. Madiah went on to become a Lt Col and he commanded 6 Kumaon in the 1962 war.
7. Captain Sukhdarshan Singh went on to become a Major and he was second-in-command of 13 Kumaon in 1961.
8. Captain S.L. Sharma went on to become a Lt Col and he commanded 14 Kumaon.
9. Lieutenant Jaswant Singh went on to become a Major and he was transferred to 13 Kumaon.

10. Lieutenant Lakha Singh went on to become a Lt Col and he commanded 4 Kumaon in the 1971 war.
11. Second Lieutenant I.R. Kumar went on to become a Major General, he commanded 5 Kumaon. He died while on active duty.
12. Sepoy Man Singh retired as a Subedar/Honorary Captain. He participated in the 1962 war and was one of the few survivors of the Delta Company of 6 Kumaon in the Battle of Walong.

Kumaon Regimental Centre

1. Lieutenant Colonel N.K. Sinha went on to become a Colonel and he commanded Kumaon Regimental Centre thrice.
2. Lieutenant Colonel Ram Singh retired and settled in Jaipur, he died at the age of 102 in 2019.
3. Major Mohar Singh went on to become a Lt Col and he commanded 5 Kumaon.
4. Major T.S. Samra, his records couldn't be found.
5. Major S.C. Suri, his records couldn't be found.
6. Captain M.K. Sheriff, his records couldn't be found.
7. Captain N.A. Sallick, VrC went on to command 4 Kumaon and he retired as a Brigadier.
8. Captain N. Vishwanathan commanded 16 Kumaon and went on to become a Major General.
9. Lieutenant P.C. Mehta went on to become a Lt Col and he commanded 2 Kumaon.
10. Recruit Chamu Singh Mehra retired as an Honorary Captain; he also participated in the 1962 War with 6 Kumaon.

23 Infantry Division

1. Major General Bikram Singh commanded 181 Independent Brigade Group, 23 Infantry Division and 15 Corps in all the formations Shaitan Singh served under him. He died in a helicopter crash in November 1963 in Poonch.
2. Lieutenant Colonel D.S. Sidhu, his records couldn't be found.
3. Captain Magni Ram commanded 15 Dogra and died during service as a Lt Col.

13 Kumaon

1. Lieutenant Colonel B.S. Chand, VrC went on to become a Brigadier.
2. Lieutenant Colonel H.S. Dhingra, AVSM went on to become a Colonel and served at NDA before retiring.
3. Major Mukut Singh became a Lt Col and commanded 13 Kumaon from 1965-1969.
4. Major C.P.S. Chaudhari became a Lt Col and raised 11 Kumaon in 1964
5. Major J.N. Kunzru went on to become a Lt Col and he commanded 8 Kumaon.
6. Major G.N. Sinha went on to become a Major General and he commanded 3 Kumaon Rifles.
7. Major H.N. Sur retired from the Army in 1962. He wanted to join TA but later he joined a government department and he was murdered in 1963 when he caught and complained about a corrupt officer.
8. Major Gadigeppa Halgali retired from the Army and his son joined the Army and retired as a Lieutenant General.
9. Captain Hari Singh Chauhan became a Major and his further records couldn't be found.

10. Captain E.D. Wayte, his records couldn't be found except he served with 14 J&K Militia before the 1962 War.
11. Major Raghunath V. Jatar, he served with 13 Kumaon in Mizo Hills as well as commanded the unit in the 1971 war. Later he became a Brigadier and retired as Deputy GOC 3 Division.
12. Captain D.D. Saklani went on to become a Lt Gen he commanded 8 Kumaon and as a Lt Gen he remained commandant of Infantry School, Mhow.
13. Captain R.K. Khanna retired as a Major General he commanded 16 Kumaon.
14. Captain B.S. Lamba retired as a Brigadier and he commanded 15 Kumaon.
15. Lieutenant Prem Kumar retired as a Brigadier and he commanded 16 Kumaon.
16. Lieutenant P.M. Wakhle retired as a Major. He remained with 13 Kumaon till his retirement.

Others

1. Captain S.P. Dua commanded 5 Jat and retired as a Colonel.
2. Captain K.S. Kang retired as a Brigadier.
3. Lieutenant Prem Singh of 5 Jat retired as a Lt Col.
4. Lieutenant A.O. Alexander went on to raise and command 27 Madras. He was killed in the 1971 war while commanding the unit.
5. Lieutenant D. Thamboo went on to command 7 Kumaon and he retired as a Brigadier.

❑

Appendix- III

Military Terminologies

1. Troop: A soldier is called a Troop.
2. Section: A group of 10 soldiers led by a Lance Naik or Naik or a Havildar.
3. Platoon: It comprises three sections: it is commanded by a JCO or a subaltern.
4. Company: It comprises three platoons and other support elements like the Mortar section. It is commanded by a Major or a Captain, sometimes a Lieutenant also commands a company.
5. Battalion: It is an infantry unit which consists of close to eight hundred to nine hundred soldiers. It is divided into four rifle companies Alpha, Bravo, Charlie and Delta and two administration companies Support and Headquarters company. It also has support elements like mortar platoon, signals platoon, motorised transport platoon, etc. Nowadays battalions are commanded by full Colonels but till the late 1980s all battalions were commanded by Lieutenant Colonels.
6. Brigade: Three to four battalions form a brigade. It is commanded by a Brigadier.

7. Division: Three to four brigades with support elements comprise a division. It is commanded by a Major General.

8. Corps: Two or three divisions comprise a Corps. Corps is commanded by a Lieutenant General.

9. Command: Many corps put together comprise the entire command. It includes various elements of infantry, artillery, cavalry, services, signals, aviation, etc. There are seven commands in the Indian Army. Army Command is commanded by a Lieutenant General who has already commanded a corps and is senior in hierarchy.

10. Army : All seven commands comprise the whole Army. The Army is commanded by a General, also called COAS.

❑

Names of Martyrs

S.No	IC/Army No	Rank & Name
1	IC-6400	MAJ SHAITAN SINGH BHATI, PVC
2	JC-20355	Jem RAM YADAV, VrC
3	4134106	NK SINGHRAM YADAV, VrC
4	4140983	NK GULAB SINGH YADAV,VrC
5	4140476	NK HUKUM CHAND YADAV,VrC
6	6792413	NURSING ASST DHARAMPAL DAHIYA, VrC
7	JC18192	JAMADAR HARIRAM YADAV, VrC
8	4132526	CHM HARPHOOL SINGH YADAV, SM
9	4133193	HAV RAMNARAYAN YADAV
10	4138037	HAV TARA CHAND YADAV
11	4139185	DEVI SAHAY YADAV
12	4139579	SEP LAL SINGH YADAV
13	4141690	SEP CHAMAN LAL YADAV
14	4141817	SEP DHARAM SINGH YADAV
15	4139287	SEP DEVI SAHAY YADAV
16	4142021	SEP SHRI CHAND YADAV
17	4140265	NK RAMSWAROOP YADAV
18	4142290	SEP MAHENDRA SINGH YADAV
19	4142875	SEP DHARAM PAL YADAV
20	4144819	COOK SHYODAN BABRIYA
21	4143750	SEP RAMKUMAR YADAV
22	4143783	SEP SHER SINGH YADAV

23	4143826	SEP RAM SINGH YADAV
24	4144668	SEP PHOOL SINGH YADAV
25	4145196	SEP SOORAJ SINGH BHAN YADAV
26	4144983	SEP PYARELAL YADAV
27	4145340	SEP JAI SINGH YADAV
28	4146139	SEP BALBEER SINGH YADAV
29	4146264	SEP SOORAJ BHAN YADAV
30	4146719	SEP DHARAMPAL YADAV
31	4147424	SEP DEEPCHAND YADAV
32	4147426	SEP BANSHILAL YADAV
33	4131861	SEP PRABHATI LAL YADAV
34	4132273	SEP KALURAM YADAV
35	4140750	SEP MAHADEVA YADAV
36	4139430	SEP BARBAR CHAJURAM
37	4140890	LANS. NK CHANDRASHEKHAR YADAV
38	4141047	LANS NK PRATHVI SINGH YADAV
39	4141692	LANS.NK NITYANAND YADAV
40	4141801	SEP RAGHUBIR SINGH YADAV
41	4141813	SEP RAMJILAL YADAV
42	4142294	LANCE NK SHRI RAM YADAV
43	4146104	SEP SHER SINGH YADAV
44	4146328	SEP PHOOL SINGH YADAV
45	4147092	SEP RAMESHWAR YADAV
46	4147474	SEP GYANSINGH YADAV
47	4147080	SEP LAXMI NARAYAN YADAV
48	4128494	NK BHOOP SINGH YADAV
49	4128045	HAV ROOP CHAND YADAV
50	4141987	SEP RAM MEHAR YADAV
51	4142146	NK ROOPRAM YADAV
52	4143147	SEP RANJEET SINGH YADAV

53	4143551	SEP BHARAT SINGH YADAV
54	4146420	SEP AASHA RAM YADAV
55	4145693	SEP MEER SINGH YADAV
56	4131998	NK SOORAT SINGH YADAV
57	4133423	SEP DOOLICHAND YADAV
58	4135884	NK CHANDGIRAM YADAV
59	4139564	SEP ROOGHNATH SINGH YADAV
60	2943555	NK SAHIRAM YADAV
61	4145044	SEP SHER SINGH YADAV
62	4146106	SEP RATAN SINGH YADAV
63	4144049	SEP RAMPHAL
64	4131441	HAV RAMANAND YADAV
65	4132950	SEP BRIJLAL YADAV
66	4140577	NK RAMJILAL YADAV
67	4141584	SEP SULTAN SINGH YADAV
68	4143538	SEP RAMDAYAL YADAV
69	4145343	SEP RAMSINGH YADAV
70	4144219	SEP AMILAL YADAV
71	4146012	SEP SHRAVAN KUMAR YADAV
72	4146093	SEP JAGMAL SINGH YADAV
73	4145258	LANCE NK HARIRAM YADAV
74	4146159	SEP KHOOBRAM YADAV
75	4146269	SEP DAYARAM YADAV
76	4146273	SEP PRABHOO YADAV
77	4147510	SEP PHHOL SINGH YADAV
78	4147520	SEP TARA CHAND YADAV
79	4147524	SEP RAMJILAL YADAV
80	4147541	SEP HARI RAM YADAV
81	4147542	SEP RAMKANWAR YADAV
82	4146111	SEP MEHARCHAND YADAV
83	4133638	SEP RAMDEO YADAV

84	4144131	SEP RAMKUNWAR YADAV
85	4143815	SEP GIRDHARI YADAV
86	4134057	HAV BALBEER SINGH YADAV
87	4143499	SEP SOORAJ NATH SINGH YADAV
88	4145729	SEP TILAKDHARI YADAV
89	4144743	SEP KRISHN MURARI YADAV
90	4140470	NK LALU RAM YADAV
91	4143180	SEP GAYADIN YADAV
92	4143344	SEP JAGDHAR SINGH YADAV
93	4146199	SEP BABU SINGH YADAV
94	4144233	SEP KIRAN SINGH YADAV
95	4146085	SEP RAMPHAL SINGH YADAV
96	4145587	SEP SULTAN SINGH YADAV
97	4145979	SEP HARISH CHANDRA YADAV
98	4145515	SEP KHEMKARAN YADAV
99	4147039	SEP UDAIVEER YADAV
100	4143598	LANCE NK DAYARAM YADAV
101	4147173	SEP KISHAN YADAV
102	4147811	SEP RAMSWAROOP YADAV
103	4147809	SEP RAHIMAL YADAV
104	4145623	SEP RAJBAHADUR YADAV
105	4145623	SEP SHEETALA PRASAD YADAV
106	4146077	SEP SATYADEO YADAV
107	4144229	SEP CHANDRA PATI YADAV
108	4144573	SEP CHANDRA BHAN YADAV
109	4147067	SEP BISHVANATH YADAV
110	4134027	SEP SAFAI KARAMCHARI BAHAR

Abbreviations

1. Gen - General
2. Lt Gen - Lieutenant General
3. Maj Gen - Major General
4. Brig - Brigadier
5. Col - Colonel
6. Lt Col - Lieutenant Colonel
7. Maj - Major
8. Capt - Captain
9. Lt - Lieutenant
10. 2/Lt - Second Lieutenant
11. Hony Capt - Honorary Captain
12. Hony Lt - Honorary Lieutenant
13. Sub Maj - Subedar Major
14. Sub - Subedar
15. Jem - Jemadar/Nb Sub - Naib Subedar
16. Hav - Havildar
17. Nk - Naik
18. L/Nk - Lance Naik
19. Sep - Sepoy
20. Inf - Infantry

21. Div - Division
22. Bde - Brigade
23. Indp Bde Grp - Independent Brigade Group
24. Bn - Battalion
25. Coy - Company
26. Pl - Platoon
27. Sec - Section
28. IMA - Indian Military Academy
29. OTS - Officers Training School
30. OTA - Officers Training Academy
31. NDA - National Defence Academy
32. GOC - General Officer Commanding
33. Bde Cdr - Brigade Commander
34. CO - Commanding Officer
35. 2-IC - Second in Command
36. GSO - General Staff Officer
37. Adjt - Adjutant
38. QM - Quartermaster
39. Coy Cdr - Company Commander
40. Pl Cdr - Platoon Commander
41. IO - Intelligence Officer
42. JCO - Junior Commissioned Officer
43. NCO - Non Commissioned Officer
44. CHM - Company Havildar Major
45. CQMH - Company Quartermaster Havildar

46. TA - Technical Assistant
47. NCSE – Non-Combatants (Enrolled)
48. PVC - Paramvir Chakra
49. MVC - Mahavir Chakra
50. VrC - Vir Chakra
51. AC - Ashoka Chakra
52. VSM - Vishisht Seva Medal
53. SM - Sena Medal
54. M-in-D - Mention in Despatches
55. MC - Military Cross
56. MBE - Member of Order of British Empire
57. DSO - Distinguished Service Order
58. OBI - Order of British India
59. MM - Military Medal
60. OP - Observation Post
61. LP - Listening Post
62. HMG - Heavy Machine Gun
63. MMG - Medium Machine Gun
64. LMG - Light Machine Gun
65. RCL Gun - Recoilless Gun

❑